Sampling the PSALMS

Sampling the PSALMS

BY

HENRY M. MORRIS, Ph.D.

CREATION-LIFE PUBLISHERS

San Diego, California

Sampling the Psalms

Copyright © 1978
CREATION-LIFE PUBLISHERS
P.O. Box 15666
San Diego, California 92115

Library of Congress Catalog Card Number 78-55613
ISBN 0-89051-049-0

Library of Congress Cataloging in Publication Data
Morris, Henry Madison, 1918-
   Sampling the Psalms.
   1. Bible. O.T. Psalms English—Commentaries. I. Title.
BS1430.M76   223.2   78-55613
ISBN 0-89051-049-0

Printed in United States of America

Cover by Marvin Ross

Printed by
El Camino Press
La Verne, Calif.

CONTENTS

INTRODUCTION

The book of Psalms has been a delight and blessing to the people of God for a hundred generations. In more ways than one, it is at the very heart of the Bible. The central chapter of the Bible is Psalm 117, which is also the shortest chapter in the Bible. The next chapter contains the central verse of the Bible, Psalm 118:8, which affirms very appropriately that: "It is better to trust in the Lord than to put confidence in man." Then the next chapter, Psalm 119, is the longest and most amazing chapter in the Bible (see page 142).

But more importantly, the book of Psalms is the heart of the Bible in that it speaks to our own hearts more eloquently and fervently than does any other book. It is the book of praise, the book of singing — but also the book of comfort and even sometimes the book of anger. It is a book of testimony and a book of prayer; it speaks of joy in the midst of sorrow and hope in the midst of despair.

In our own family devotionals, extending now every day through the past thirty-eight years, the Scripture readings have been from the book of Psalms more than from any other book of the Bible. Speaking personally (and, no doubt many other Christians would agree), although I love and try to study all the Bible, the book of Psalms is my *favorite* book!

I believe that the book of Genesis is the most *important* book of the Bible, since it is the foundation of all the rest. Similarly the book of Revelation is the most thrilling book of the Bible, because it is the climax of all the rest, ushering us into the very vestibule of eternity.

Nevertheless, the book of Psalms is my favorite, because here I experience more direct communion between my own heart and the heart of God than anywhere else in Scripture.

A verse-by-verse study of any of the psalms inevitably yields a great harvest of spiritual blessing. They are far more than mere devotional poems for pious reading. Each contains depths of revelation that seem inexhaustible. Furthermore, there are probably more direct and concrete marks of divine inspiration in the Psalms than in any other book. There are numerous scientific insights far in advance of their discovery by scientists, many amazingly-fulfilled prophecies of the coming Savior, and even many evidences of remarkable geometric structure in the very combinations of words and concepts, that are inexplicable except in terms of inspiration by the Holy Spirit.

This book is written with the purpose of sharing with others some of the blessings I have experienced in studying the marvelous book of Psalms. There are, of course, 150 chapters in the entire book of Psalms, and I have only covered a fraction of them in this particular book. The ones discussed, however, are among the most remarkable psalms, both in their evidences of divine inspiration and in their impact on our hearts and souls as we study them. The exposition of these, hopefully, will encourage others to devote similar studies of their own to all the other psalms as well.

After an introductory section, dealing with an overview of the book of Psalms and an analysis of the first Psalm, I have tried to provide a fairly detailed exposition of a number of psalms which bear on various aspects of modern science. Most of these chapters were originally broadcast on our I.C.R.* radio program, "Science, Scripture, and Salvation."

---

*Institute for Creation Research. For information, write I.C.R., 2716 Madison Avenue, San Diego, California, 92116.

A third section deals in some depth with several of the more important Messianic psalms. These contain a number of amazing prophecies fulfilled a thousand years later in the person and work of the Lord Jesus Christ.

The Christian life, from beginning to end, is the theme of the next section, focusing on the series of 15 remarkable psalms known as the Songs of Degrees. Finally, the last section features the grand Epilogue to the book of Psalms, the great Hallelujah songs in its final five chapters.

The beauty of the Psalms is brought out most effectively in the King James translation, and this is the translation followed herein. I would urge the reader to have his King James Bible open at the appropriate psalm as he reads this book, following the passage concurrently with the exposition. In most cases, the study proceeds verse-by-verse (or at least section-by-section), and continual reference to the psalm itself is essential for maximum benefit.

I can only hope that these studies—admittedly making a somewhat unusual approach to the exposition of this tremendous book—will yield as much blessing to the reader as they have to the writer. As we proceed to the study, there are no words more appropriate than those of the Psalmist himself:

I will worship toward thy holy temple; and praise thy name for thy lovingkindness and for thy truth: for thou hast magnified thy word above all thy name (Psalm 138:2).

PART ONE

MESSAGE AND METHOD IN THE PSALMS

Chapter 1

SONGS IN THE NIGHT

The book of Psalms is unique in the Bible. It was the hymnbook of Israel and, to a great extent, has been the pattern for all the other hymnbooks used by God's people through the ages. The Jews call it "The Hallal Book"—"The Book of Praises." It is replete with songs of praise, of course, but it also contains a strong component of songs of suffering, songs of battle, and even songs of imprecation.

The word for "psalms" (Hebrew *mizmer*) means "songs," probably implying songs which were to be sung with musical accompaniment. Most of them were written originally by David, but some had other authors (even Moses) and many are anonymous. They were collected by some unknown process of selection into five Books, with a total of 150 psalms comprising 2,461 verses in all.

THE THEME OF CONFLICT

Although the note of praise does sound often in the psalms, the theme of spiritual warfare is even more frequent. In almost every psalm (only Psalms 100, 133, and

150 seem to be exceptions) the element of conflict is
either implicit or explicit. The great conflict of the ages
is the struggle between truth and deception, between sin
and righteousness, between the godly and ungodly, between the chosen nation and the heathen, and finally between God and Satan.

The first Psalm contains the definitive statement on
this conflict and is the foundation for all the other
psalms. The final Psalm (150) speaks of the final and
eternal victory of God and His purposes. This victory is
foreshadowed in the first Psalm, but the conflict is very
real throughout all the intervening psalms.

It is singularly appropriate, of course, for a book
whose theme is songs of praise to be also a book of warfare and struggle and suffering. This present world is
groaning and travailing together in pain (Romans 8:22),
and "man is born unto trouble, as the sparks fly upward" (Job 5:7).

But it is trust in God that enables the believer to be
joyful in spite of trouble. "As unknown, and yet well
known; as dying, and, behold, we live; as chastened, and
not killed; as sorrowful, yet always rejoicing; as poor, yet
making many rich; as having nothing, and yet possessing all things" (II Corinthians 6:9, 10).

Such is the note sounded throughout the Psalms. The
world is in darkness, but the light of God's promises continually illumines the way. "Deep calleth unto deep at
the noise of thy waterspouts: all thy waves and thy bil-
lows are gone over me. Yet the Lord will command His
lovingkindness in the daytime and in the night His song
shall be with me, and my prayer unto the God of my
life" (Psalm 42:7, 8).

It is significant that the first actual reference to singing in the Psalms is in the verse immediately following
the first of the so-called "imprecations" in the Psalms.
Note the contrast: "Destroy thou them, O God; let them
fall by their own counsels; cast them out in the multitude of their transgressions; for they have rebelled
against thee. But let all those that put their trust in thee

rejoice; let them ever shout for joy [same as "sing for joy"], because thou defendest them: let them also that love thy name be joyful in thee" (Psalm 5:11).

STRUCTURE OF THE BOOK OF PSALMS

The book of Psalms actually consists of five "books," composed as follows:

Book	I.	Psalms	1 through	41	=	41 psalms
Book	II.	Psalms	42 through	72	=	31 psalms
Book	III.	Psalms	73 through	89	=	17 psalms
Book	IV.	Psalms	90 through	106	=	17 psalms
Book	V.	Psalms	107 through	145	=	39 psalms
Epilogue		Psalms	146 through	150	=	5 psalms

Book of Psalms   = 150 psalms

No one knows the original reason for the compilations as listed. Probably they represent ancient chronological and/or thematic compilations, but the details are obscure. Most Bibles indicate the last five psalms to have been a part of Book V but, for reasons to be discussed in the last section, it appears more likely that they are intended as a grand epilogue to the entire five books.

The ancient Jewish commentators believed the five groupings corresponded to the five books of Moses, the "Pentateuch." Any supposed correlation in subject matter based on this idea seems quite tenuous, however.

Authors named in the traditional inscriptions on the psalms may account in part for the collections. For example, Book I consists almost entirely of Davidic psalms and so may represent the first collection of his father's psalms as published by Solomon. Altogether, seven different authors are found listed in these inscriptions, but fully a third of the psalms carry no name. Authorship is divided among the various books in accordance with the following tabulation.

Author	Book I	Book II	Book III	Book IV	Book V	Epilogue	Total
David	37	18	1	2	15		73
Asaph		1	11				12
Sons of Korah		7	3				10
Moses				1			1
Solomon		1			1		2
Heman			1				1
Ethan			1				1
Anonymous	4	4		14	23	5	50
Total	41	31	17	17	39	5	150

Actually, one of the anonymous psalms in Book I (Psalm 2) is attributed to David in Acts 4:25, and Psalm 72, called "A Psalm of Solomon," closes with the words, "The prayers of David the son of Jesse are ended," so that it may have been written by David instead of Solomon. Also, Psalm 127 is called "A Song of Degrees *for* Solomon," and the eleven psalms attributed to the Sons of Korah were actually inscribed as "*for* the Sons of Korah." Thus the total may, with these revisions, become somewhat more symmetrical.

Author	Book I	Book II	Book III	Book IV	Book V	Epilogue	Total
David	38	19	1	2	15		75
Asaph		1	11				12
Moses				1			1
Heman			1				1
Ethan			1				1
Anonymous	3	11	3	14	24	5	60
Total	41	31	17	17	39	5	150

Many of the "anonymous" psalms, of course, may well have been written by David or one of the other psalmists listed above.

One significant feature of the five books is that each ends with a great doxology. These are:

I. *Psalm 41:13.* "Blessed be the Lord God of Israel from everlasting, and to everlasting. Amen and amen."

II. *Psalm 72:19.* "And blessed be His glorious name forever: and let the whole earth be filled with His glory: Amen and Amen."

III. *Psalm 89:52.* "Blessed be the Lord for evermore. Amen and Amen."

IV. *Psalm 106:48.* "Blessed be the Lord God of Israel from everlasting to everlasting: and let all the people say Amen. Praise ye the Lord."

V. *Psalm 145:21.* "My mouth shall speak the praise of the Lord; and let all flesh bless His holy name for ever and ever."

The Epilogue ends not with a similar "blessing," but with an even greater exhortation and doxology:

Let every thing that hath breath praise the Lord. Praise ye the Lord (Psalm 150:6).

Just prior to each of these grand book-ending doxologies, however, had been a testimony of great conflict with the enemies of God and God's people. Psalm 145:20 is representative: "The Lord preserveth all them that love Him: but all the wicked will He destroy."

Such is the book of Psalms — God's gracious assurances to all who love Him in the midst of a sinful world, to the accompaniment of their praises and their songs in the night.

Chapter 2

THE TWO WAYS AND THE TWO DESTINIES
(Psalm 1)

THE FOUNDATION PSALM

The first Psalm is an introductory psalm, laying the foundation for all the others. Appropriately, its author is anonymous, but he outlines in graphic language the great theme of the age-long conflict between the ungodly and the righteous, with their two ends. The first three verses describe the way of the righteous man and the last three verses the way of the ungodly. The righteous will be sustained in the midst of an ungodly world, but the ungodly will ultimately be destroyed in the judgment.

Though men commonly claim there are many ways and all lead to God, the Scriptures make it clear from beginning to end that there are only *two* ways, one leading to heaven and one to hell. The Lord Jesus made this fact forever clear: "Enter ye in at the strait gate: for wide is the gate, and broad is the way, that leadeth to destruction; and many there be which go in thereat. Because strait is the gate, and narrow is the way which leadeth unto life, and few there be that find it" (Matthew 7:13, 14).

The two ways and the two destinies constitute the theme of innumerable other Scriptures. For example:

And I will put enmity between thee and the woman, and between thy seed and her seed; it shall bruise thy head, and thou shalt bruise his heel (Genesis 3:15).

And many of them that sleep in the dust of the earth shall awake, some to everlasting life, and some to shame and everlasting contempt (Daniel 12:2).

Then shall ye return, and discern between the righteous and the wicked, between him that serveth God and him that serveth Him not (Malachi 3:18).

Marvel not at this: for the hour is coming, in the which all that are in the graves shall hear His voice, and shall come forth; they that have done good, unto the resurrection of life; and they that have done evil, unto the resurrection of damnation (John 5:28, 29).

[God] will render to every man according to his deeds: to them who by patient continuance in well doing seek for glory and honour and immortality, eternal life; but unto them that are contentious, and do not obey the truth, but obey unrighteousness, indignation and wrath, tribulation and anguish, upon every soul of man that doeth evil (Romans 2:6-9).

The conflict has many faces and forms. Behind it all is the primeval and continuing Satanic rebellion against God. Satan has gained dominion over the world once given to Adam, and this will continue until God's final victory over him at the end of the age. In the interim, God through Christ has paid the price of redemption and is recovering many souls from the snare of the devil, their salvation being accomplished through their faith in His Word. The spiritual battle rages primarily now in the minds of men, who must decide between "the counsel of the ungodly" and "the law of the Lord" (verses 1 and 2), but this decision of the mind and will has all manner of consequences in life and character.

The counsel of the ungodly is nothing less than the philosophy of the natural man who seeks to understand his existence and control his destiny without regard to God. It is man-centered rather than God-centered, humanistic rather than theistic, based on the myth of evolution instead of the fact of creation. Standing in stark contrast is the infallible Word of God, revealing the Lord as sovereign Creator and Judge, and man as hopelessly lost without God's salvation.

THE WAY OF THE RIGHTEOUS
(Verses 1-3)

The psalm begins with the wonderful word "Blessed." This word (Hebrew *ashere*) means "happy" and is often so translated. It occurs in the book of Psalms more than in all the rest of the Bible put together. Thus, even though the theme of conflict is prominent throughout the psalms, they begin on a note of happiness and end (Psalm 150:6) on a note of praise.

We do not know who wrote this psalm, although most of the psalms in Book I (Psalms 1-41) were written by David. Its terminology (particularly the word "scornful") is unique to this particular psalm, perhaps seeming more appropriate for the book of Proverbs than the book of Psalms. Possibly it was originally written by Solomon as an introduction to the first compilation of his father's writings. In any case, these first verses constitute a marvelous testimony of assurance. If one desires happiness, here is the key.

Verse one indicates the separation of the happy man from the broad way leading to destruction, while verse two describes his commitment to the narrow way leading to life. Note the progression in verse one — "walketh not," — "nor standeth" — "nor sitteth." This corresponds to the progression of commitment to the humanistic world-view. First the unwary soul would hearken to the "counsel of the ungodly;" then, he would begin to associate with "the way of sinners;" finally, he would settle down permanently in "the seat of the scornful." This is always the order. First one is impressed by the high-sounding philosophy of ungodly intellectuals; then, having rejected God's truth, he falls away from God's standard of righteousness in practice, and in the end, he assumes an attitude of scoffing superiority to all who believe God, becoming one who himself offers the "counsel of the ungodly" to those who have neglected God's Word.

Such a pathway, however attractive it may seem to the natural man, can never produce true happiness. "There is a way which seemeth right unto a man, but the end thereof are the ways of death" (Proverbs 14:12). The way of the ungodly shall perish.

Happy is the man who, despite the inducements of temporal acclaim or wealth or pleasure, refuses to be intimidated by the humanistic, naturalistic, evolutionistic wisdom of this world — "the counsel of the ungodly" — and who, instead, takes his knowledge and counsel from God in His Word. "Happy is that people, that is in such a case: yea, happy is that people, whose God is the Lord" (Psalm 144:15).

Such a man is characterized by love for the Scriptures. "His delight is in the law [Hebrew torah] of the Lord." The "law" was essentially the only part of the Scriptures then available to the psalmist, whereas we today have the complete revelation of God, and therefore far greater reason to delight in it even than he had. Furthermore, this godly man meditates in the law day and night — not that he never thinks of anything else, but rather that all his thoughts and actions are governed by his deliberate desire to be obedient to God's Word in every way. No doubt his terminology was inspired by the testimony of Joshua, with which the psalmist was familiar: "This book of the law shall not depart out of thy mouth: but thou shalt meditate therein day and night, that thou mayst observe to do all that is written therein; for then thou shalt make thy way prosperous, and then thou shalt have good success" (Joshua 1:8).

It is noteworthy that the Scriptures are set in direct confutation of the counsel of the ungodly. This is a very necessary truth for us to learn today. Ungodly counsel, sinful ways, and a scornful heart may be answered and corrected not by human wisdom and good resolutions, but only by the Word of God!

The godly man is also likened to a deep-rooted tree growing along a natural watercourse, whose leaves never wither because of drought and whose fruit is produced regularly and abundantly. The "rivers of water" may speak of the Holy Spirit (John 7:38, 39) and the "bringing forth of fruit in season" of the godly life and productive witness produced in that man by the Spirit (John 15:16; Ephesians 5:9) through the Word. As God had promised to Joshua, such a man would prosper in all he set out to do — because, of course, all of his undertakings would be directed by the Lord. "In all thy ways, acknowledge Him, and He shall direct thy paths" (Proverbs 3:6).

In contrast to the tree of the righteous, the tree of the wicked is described in Psalm 37:35, 36: "I have seen the wicked in great power, and spreading himself like a green bay tree. Yet he passed away, and, lo, he was not; yea, I sought him, but he could not be found." The second half of Psalm 1 focuses on the ungodly man.

THE WAY OF THE UNGODLY (Verses 4-6)

The grain was commonly flayed on the summit of a high and windy hill, so that the lighter chaff could be easily separated. The psalmist used such wind-driven chaff to illustrate how the ungodly would one day vanish from the earth. Though ungodly philosophies, all centered in evolutionary humanism, now spread themselves abroad in great power, like a green bay tree, they will soon pass away and never be found again. The day is coming when all ungodliness will be revealed for what it is. "And then shall that Wicked be revealed, whom the Lord shall consume with the spirit of His mouth, and shall destroy with the brightness of His coming." (II Thessalonians 2:8). Even now, in the minds and hearts of right-thinking people, such systems quickly dissipate in the light of God's Word.

Of course, it should not be forgotten that all of us are among the "ungodly" until redeemed by Christ. None are truly in "the way of the righteous." "There is none righteous; no, not one" (Romans 3:10). All were originally "in the way of sinners," because "all have sinned and come short of the glory of God" (Romans 3:23).

We were all ungodly people, but "when we were yet without strength, in due time Christ died for the ungodly" (Romans 5:6). Though we could in no way ever earn salvation, "to him that worketh not, but believeth on Him that justifieth the ungodly, his faith is counted for righteousness" (Romans 4:5). Even though we could never find and follow the way of the righteous ourselves, Jesus said: "I am the way" (John 14:6), so when we are "in Christ," we are indeed on the way of the righteous. In fact, Christ is not only the Way but He also is the very personification of righteousness. He is "Jesus Christ the righteous" (I John 2:1), and He is made righteousness unto us (I Corinthians 1:30; II Corinthians 5:21). In the final analysis, the battle is the Lord's. Jesus Christ is the ultimate Righteous One; the AntiChrist is the ultimate Ungodly one. In fact, the word "ungodly" in Psalm 1 is the same word as "wicked," and the final great Anti-Christ is "that Wicked one" in II Thessalonians 2:8.

Since Christ is not only "the Way of the Righteous," but also will be the Judge (John 5:22), it is clear that "the ungodly shall not stand in the judgment." The "great congregation" of the redeemed cannot include any who are unrepentant and therefore still among the ungodly. There will finally have to be an eternal separation of the wheat from the chaff. "The wicked shall be turned into hell, and all the nations that forget God" (Psalm 9:17).

"For the Lord knoweth the way of the righteous, but the way of the ungodly shall perish." This climactic verse of the first Psalm thus becomes the key verse of the entire Book of Psalms. Though the heathen rage and earth's leaders seek to break the rule of God and His Christ (see the second Psalm!), the way of the ungodly shall perish. Therefore, for all eternity, "Blessed is the man who walketh not in the counsel of the ungodly," and, furthermore, "Happy are all they that put their trust in Him" (Psalm 2:12).

PART TWO

MODERN SCIENCE IN ANCIENT PSALMS

Chapter 3

MAN AND THE UNIVERSE
(Psalm 8)

One of the greatest concerns of scientists and philosophers throughout the ages has been that of the nature and meaning of the physical universe and, in particular, the role of man in the universe. The Psalms often deal with this theme and, of course, ascribe it all to God. For example, the eighth Psalm begins and ends with the great testimony of praise: "O Lord our Lord [two names of God, *Jehovah*, our *Adonai*], how excellent is thy name in all the earth!" The dual name suggests that God is both Father and Son, and the occasion for praise is that God has come to earth as Son of Man as well as Son of God.

THE VASTNESS OF THE HEAVENS
(Verses 1-4)

The Book of Psalms, as we have noted before, is primarily a book of praise, and these praises often center upon the vast expanses of the heavens and upon the One who could create such an infinite, intricate cosmos. And, of course, no matter how great may be the universe, the glory of God is far above the glory of the heavens. The Cause must be greater than the Effect!

Furthermore, there are other components of the creation which even themselves are greater than the physical cosmos. Those who can praise God for His excellent name are greater. Those who can praise God in true sincerity (babes and sucklings) are greater even than those who can praise in eloquence. Such praise is "perfected praise" (see the quotation from verse 2 in Matthew 21:16 and the commentary in Matthew 11:25).

We do not yet know what purpose God may have for the stars of heaven. The nearest star is 30 trillion miles away from the earth, and it is futile to hope that men in this life will ever be able to travel to the stars in spaceships. The heavens are "thy heavens;" "the heavens are the Lord's; the earth hath He given to the children of men" (Psalm 115:16). One important purpose for the visible stars, at least, is to serve "for signs and seasons, for days and years" (Genesis 1:14).

However, man has corrupted the meaning and purpose of the stars in two ways. In one, he has assumed the stars have direct influence over human lives and has developed a monstrous system of pagan astrology. In the other, as his concept of the vastness of space has increased, he has assumed that man is of no importance; the earth is merely a speck of dust in an infinite evolving universe, and man is an accidental bit of organic scum on the dust particle.

This twentieth-century question was raised in essence long ago by the psalmist. How could the God who created the mighty heavens possibly be interested in man?

In the very question, however, divine inspiration impelled the psalmist to anticipate God's ultimate testimony to the importance of the earth and of man's life on earth — namely, that He, Himself, would become man on earth. Not only does he ask, "What is man?" but also, "What is the son of man, that thou visitest him?" The verb, "visit," is the same as "number" or "acknowledge." In some unique way, the "son of man" is acknowledged, or counted, by God on behalf of "man," of whom He is still "mindful."

This is the first time in Scripture when the term "son of man" is used, but it is far from the last! The Lord Jesus applied it to Himself no less than 80 times, beginning with Matthew 8:20 ("the Son of Man hath not where to lay His head"). This passage (verses 4-6) is quoted in the New Testament (Hebrews 2:6-8; I Corinthians 15:27) and applied to Christ, so there is no doubt that the primary meaning is Messianic and prophetic.

Far from being of no importance, the earth and man are so central in God's purposes that God had from eternity planned to come to earth and become a man Himself, in the person of His Son. Furthermore, when the earth is finally purged and made new, the Lord Jesus will dwell here on this earth forever (Revelation 21:1-3, 22-27). There is no other star or planet in the universe whose importance to God is comparable to that of the earth.

Even man in the strict biological sense is infinitely more complex than the stars, of course. It is absurd to belittle man simply because of his size. Although a star is big, it is very simple, composed mostly of hydrogen and helium. The measure of significance in the universe is not size, but order and complexity, and the human brain is by far the most complex aggregation of matter in the universe so far as science can determine. In the strictly physical sense, the earth is the most complex aggregation of inanimate matter about which we know in the universe, and it is uniquely designed as man's home.

LOWER THAN THE ANGELS
(Verse 5)

In amplifying the question, "What is man?," the psalmist notes that he has been made "lower than the angels." Evolutionists believe man is merely an animal that has evolved "higher than the apes," but such a notion is absurd. Never has any creature been found or any fossil been found of any animal which is partially man and partially ape (or part man and part anything else), although many fossils of both apes and men have been discovered. There is no scientific evidence whatever that man was not created as man, in the image of God, exactly as the Bible says (Genesis 1:27).

In what sense is man "lower than the angels"? Angels are "spirits," not subject to the limitations of gravitational and electromagnetic forces, whereas man *has* a spirit, bound within a "body" which is "earthy." Angels are "ministers of God," and "excel in strength" (Psalm 103:20, 21), but they are also "ministering spirits, sent forth to minister for them who shall be heirs of salvation" (Hebrews 1:14). Under the curse, man goes through physical death, and in fact, it was for "the suffering of death" that Christ, as Son of Man, was made lower than the angels (Hebrews 2:9). But man can also receive salvation, a privilege which is denied the fallen angels (II Peter 2:4; Jude 6).

The phrase, of course, applies especially to Christ as the Son of Man. Jesus, as Son of Man, must take on flesh and blood, not "the nature of angels" (Hebrews 2:14, 16), in order to die and to arise and to restore man's lost dominion. He who was the eternal Word must become flesh (John 1:14); He who was equal with God must become a bond servant (Philippians 2:7). Actually, the phrase, "a little lower than the angels," could also carry the meaning "for a little time [that is, 33 years] lower than the angels."

The word, "angels," in verse 5 is not the usual word for "angels," but rather is *elohim*, the most frequent name of God, also occasionally rendered "gods." That it really here means *angels*, however, is evident from its New Testament quotation (Hebrews 2:7). The use of this word here clearly suggests that the fallen angels are in view, those that are worshipped as "gods" in connection with the astrological religions of the heathen who worship "the moon and the stars which thou hast ordained." Christ, as Son of Man, was lower even than *these*!

But because He died and thereby conquered death, He is to be crowned with glory and honor. Those also who suffer with Him will be "found unto praise and honor and glory at the appearing of Jesus Christ" (I Peter 1:7).

MAN'S DOMINION
(Verses 6-8)

Man, created in God's image, was given dominion over all the works of God's hands, including especially the animal kingdom. The reference even to those deep-sea animals that "pass through the paths of the seas" long ago inspired the great Christian hydrographer and scientist, Matthew Maury, to find and chart these subterranean pathways, and he has for over a century been honored by mariners as the "pathfinder of the seas."

Although man was given this dominion (Genesis 1:26-28), he has never exercised it fully or faithfully, and since the Flood there has actually been enmity between man and the animals (Genesis 9:2-5). This dominion and harmony will someday be fully restored (Isaiah 11:6-9; Hosea 2:18), but only after Christ returns.

When Jesus Christ came as the Son of Man, He occasionally did manifest His authority over the animal Kingdom (Matthew 17:27), as well as the physical creation (Mark 4:41), but He had come to bear and remove the curse on the earth and so was "obedient unto death" (Philippians 2:7-11). Therefore, although God had "put all things under His feet" (verse 6), nevertheless, "now we see not yet all things put under Him" (Hebrews 2:8).

THE SON OF MAN ACKNOWLEDGED
(Verse 9)

At this point in Psalm 8, between verses 8 and 9, there is a great parenthesis. Although God had given man dominion over the earth, he had failed. Before the Son of Man could be "acknowledged" (verse 4) as having regained this dominion and thereby inherited the promises, He must pay the price to redeem it.

In this parenthesis, therefore, we must insert Hebrews 2:8, 9: "Thou hast put all things in subjection under His feet. For in that He put all in subjection under Him, He left nothing that is not put under Him. But now we see not yet all things put under Him. But we see Jesus, who was made a little lower than the angels for the suffering of death, crowned with glory and honor; that He by the grace of God should taste death for every man."

It is only after the substitutionary death of the Son of Man, followed by His victorious resurrection and His coronation at the second coming, that He will indeed reign over all the earth.

Then will He surely be acknowledged as King of Kings and Lord of Lords. Then will it finally be fitting to exclaim with the psalmist: "O Lord Jesus [*Jehovah, our Adonai*], how excellent is thy name in all the earth!"

Chapter 4
NATURAL REVELATION AND THE WRITTEN WORD
(Psalm 19)

One of the grandest objects of praise to God is that of His marvelous creation, and this theme, as noted before, is prominent in the psalms. As the psalmists sing of the wonders and beauties of the physical universe, they necessarily deal with many of the same phenomena which are the objects of study in modern science. It is significant that, as they do, their poetic expressions are always remarkably in accord with the most modern scientific descriptions of the same phenomena. Often, in fact, their insights anticipate modern science by thousands of years. One of the most remarkable of the psalms with such features is Psalm 19.

THE SPACE-MASS-TIME UNIVERSE
(Verses 1-2)

The 19th Psalm is divided into two main parts — the first six verses, discussing God's revelation through His World, and the last eight verses, stressing His even greater revelation through His Word. It begins by calling attention to the physical universe, verse one stating the testimony of Space and verse two that of Time.

Each of these two verses uses the structure of Hebrew poetic parallelism to emphasize its theme. In verse one, the terms "heavens" and "firmament" are synonymous (note Genesis 1:8 — "God called the firmament Heaven"), and both mean essentially what we mean by our modern scientific term, *Space*. Thus, the vast reaches of Space everywhere provide the backdrop, as it were, for God to "show forth His power and His work." Everywhere throughout the infinite universe occur phenomena declaring His omnipotence and His orderliness, "the glory of God, and His handiwork."

Similarly, verse two speaks of *Time*, during which ("day after day" and "night after night") the phenomena in Space perpetually yield information in unending communication between the Creator and His creation. Thus, everywhere in Space occur phenomena, energized and ordered, transmitting information eternally through *Time*.

Modern science recognizes the universe to be a *continuum* of Space, Time, and Energy (or Information), and so does this ancient Psalm! Everything that happens in Space and Time (call it an "event," a "process," a "system," or whatever) involves "power" doing "work" and "communication" transmitting "knowledge."

THE STANDARD OF MEASURE
(Verses 3-4)

This marvelous universe is always teaching about God to people of all nations. Although there is no audible voice nor written message, the lesson is freely available in all times and places. "The *invisible* things are clearly seen!" (Romans 1:20), and the inaudible words are plainly heard, so that men are "without excuse" if they fail to heed. By the simple, universal experience of cause-and-effect ("every effect must have an adequate cause") the universe teaches about the great First Cause. The cause of boundless Space and endless Time must be infinite and eternal; the cause of universal power and complex order must be omnipotent and omniscient; the communicator of needed knowledge to personal beings must be personal and gracious. Therefore, the God of Creation is an infinite, eternal, omnipotent, omniscient, personal, gracious Being!

This universal testimony is itself the divine standard which measures human response. The psalmist calls it the surveyor's "line" which goes out to "measure" the hearts of men through all the earth. That is, the manner in which a person responds to the witness of God in creation measures the very nature of his heart-attitude toward God, Himself. The Apostle Paul, answering his own rhetorical question ("But I say, have they not heard?"), quotes this very verse (see Romans 10:13-18) to prove that all men have access to the knowledge of the true God, merely through observing His creation.

The great indictment, however, is that, although "the heavens declare the glory of God," all men "come short of the glory of God" (Romans 3:23). The "line" has "gone out" to measure them, but they have not measured up. They have all "changed the glory of the incorruptible God" into a form suitable to human conceit rather than to the divine standard, and thus "God also gave them up" (Romans 1:23, 24).

THE TESTIMONY OF THE SUN
(Verses 5-6)

The greatest of the works of God in the physical creation, as far as the earth is concerned, is the sun. "In them" (that is, in Space and Time) God has established a "tent" for the sun. The sun provides all the energy for the earth's processes, doing so through its continual "going forth." This phrase does not refer mainly to the sun's daily orbit, but is a translation of a Hebrew word (used also in Micah 5:2; Deuteronomy 8:3, and Psalm 65:8) which speaks of something which goes forth from the object itself.

The reference clearly is to the sun's radiant energy, going forth from its surface as a result of unknown reactions in its depths. A part of that energy reaches the earth, where it is converted through various processes into the chemical energy of its biosphere, the electrical and kinetic energies of its atmosphere, the hydraulic energy of its rains and rivers, and all the other energy resources on which the earth subsists.

Not only does the sun's radiation energize the earth, but all the rest of the solar system. In fact, as the sun moves in a gigantic orbit through the Milky Way Galaxy (an orbit that would require 230 million years for one circuit, at a speed of 600,000 miles per hour), and the galaxy moves in an unknown path relative to the other galaxies of space, its circuit seems truly to be from one end of the heavens to the other. As its radiant energy continually goes forth, it is literally true that "there is nothing hid from the heat thereof."

As far as the earth is concerned, this physical "light of the world" provides energy for all its work, especially for the maintenance of life on its surface. These processes, drawing on the solar heat energy, must obey the laws of thermodynamics ("heat power"). It is providential, however, (and perhaps ironical, as well) that, just as God's revelation in creation both illumines and judges the human heart, so the sun both energizes and disintegrates physical and biological systems on earth. The first law of thermodynamics is the law of conservation of energy, reflecting the completion and sustenance of God's finished work of creation. The second law is the law of increasing nonavailability of energy, reflecting the curse on God's creation because of man's sin.

Both laws seem specially to be implemented by the sun. The environmental radiations cause somatic mutations, leading to the aging and death of individual organisms, and also genetic mutations, leading to the deterioration and extinction of species. Storms, erosion, rusting, and most other decay mechanisms are triggered by solar energy. And yet the sun's energy continually replenishes the earth's deteriorating energy resources. "There is nothing hid from the heat thereof."

The sun also is a beautiful type of the Lord Jesus Christ, the spiritual "light of the world" (John 8:12). The heavens declare the glory of God, and He is the very "out-raying of the glory of God" (Hebrews 1:3), "upholding all things by the word of His power." He is the Creator of all things, and therefore all created things reflect His handiwork. The sun, in its daily triumph over the darkness, emerging as a great bridegroom racing forth to rescue the darkened world and claim it as its own, continually renews God's promise of a heavenly Bridegroom who will someday save and cleanse His earthly Bride from the curse of death and darkness.

THE WRITTEN WORD (Verses 8-14)

In spite of the tremendous witness concerning God and His grace and power plainly revealed in the created cosmos, men everywhere mistake or distort or reject its message. The testimony is there, so that men are without excuse, but the testimony is not received, so that they are also without salvation.

The *world* of the Lord is imperfect in its bondage to the curse, thus condemning the souls of men, but the *Word* of the Lord is perfect, converting their souls. What natural revelation only promises, written revelation accomplishes! "The Holy Scriptures which are able to make thee wise unto salvation through faith which is in Christ Jesus" (II Timothy 3:15). They not only bring conversion, but also wisdom and joy, illumination, endurance, and righteousness. When the creation was completed, it was all "very good," but it has since been corrupted by sin and the curse. The written Word, however, despite all the attempts of men and devils to corrupt and destroy it, remains "living and powerful,"

the "incorruptible seed," the "words which will not pass
away" (Hebrews 4:12; I Peter 1:23; Matthew 24:35). The
Scriptures are perfect and sure, right and pure, clean
and true.

These very verses in Psalm 19 bespeak its divine origin
by their modern perspective on scientific truth. It is important to understand the witness of God in creation,
but far more important to understand the Word!

In verse 7, there is a remarkable eighteen-fold testimony of the nature and power of the Holy Scriptures.
Note the following outline:

THE WRITTEN WORD OF THE LORD

What it Is	What it Does	Why it Can
Law (i.e., *torah*)	Converts	Perfect
Testimony	Instructs	Sure
Statutes (or "precepts")	Rejoices	Right
Commandment	Enlightens	Pure
Fear	Endures	Clean
Judgments	Makes Righteous	True

David only had a small part of the complete Scriptures in his day, and yet he could make such statements
concerning them. Far more was available to the Apostle
Paul when he said: "All Scripture is given by inspiration
of God, and is profitable for doctrine, for reproof, for cor-
rection, for instruction in righteousness; That the man of
God may be perfect, throughly furnished unto all good
works" (II Timothy 3:16, 17).

Thus combining the testimonies of David and Paul.
"The law of the Lord is perfect . . . . that the man of
God may be perfect!" The man who knows the Scriptures is wealthier than the richest man on earth, because
they are more to be desired than much fine gold. The
most exquisite pleasures of life are nothing in comparison, for God's Word is sweeter than honey!

The Scriptures provide all necessary warning, lest we suffer loss and all necessary instruction, that we might earn great rewards. They impel us to seek cleansing even from sins of ignorance ("secret faults"), as well as to pray for strength against yielding to willful and presumptuous sins, or even the "great transgression" of final rejection of the Word of God itself. "Let them not have dominion over me," he prays, and the answer comes: "For sin shall *not* have dominion over you: for ye are not under the law, but under grace" (Romans 6:14).

The final verse is a beautiful prayer, recognizing the necessary relation between the thoughts of our hearts and the words on our lips (compare Romans 10:9, 10; Colossians 3:16; I Peter 3:15; etc.). If the Word of God is the center of both, then both will indeed be acceptable to the One who will be both Redeemer and Strong Refuge to our souls.

Chapter 5

KING AT THE
FLOOD (Psalm 29)

The 29th Psalm is often known as the "Psalm of the Voice of the Lord," because of the seven-times repeated occurrence of this phrase in its verses. Other than this rather obvious characteristic, however, the exact interpretation of the psalm has often been confusing to commentators. They have usually explained it as a poetic description by David of a great storm blowing inland from the Mediterranean Sea, but the details of this interpretation seem obscure, to say the least.

The real key to its meaning, however, is found in verse 10: "The Lord sitteth upon the flood." There are ten Hebrew words translated "flood" in the Old Testament, but the word here is *mabbul*, a word used uniquely to refer to the worldwide cataclysm in the days of Noah. In fact, this is the only place in the Bible where this word is used except in the story of the great Flood in Genesis 6-9, where it is always used. Therefore, it is certain that the writer of Psalm 29 was speaking of that great cataclysmic storm, and no other.

Probably, as David was sitting at his upper palace window one day, gazing with awe at a great storm of wind and rain blowing in from the sea, raging from Hermon and Lebanon in the north to Kadesh in the south, he felt himself translated in the Spirit backwards in time to that great cataclysm of the past. In his vision, he

saw and recorded these tremendous events accompanying the great Flood.

SONS OF THE MIGHTY (Verses 1-2)

The psalm opens with a scene in heaven, picturing a
mighty host around God's throne. The leader of the host
calls out a great exhortation to "give unto the Lord glory
and strength," addressing his appeal to "ye mighty."
The original word is a compound, *bene elim*, "sons of the
mighty." It is also used in Psalm 89:6, in a similar
setting: "For who in the heaven can be compared unto
the Lord? who among the sons of the mighty can be
likened unto the Lord?" Here the expression is *bene el*.
Both, of course, are practically identical with *bene
elohim*, translated "sons of God" in Genesis 6:1, 4.

Thus, it becomes clear that the scene depicts the
angelic "sons of God," who had been faithful to God at
the time of the great Flood, praising Him for His mighty
victory over those rebellious sons of the mighty one.
Through the vehicle of demon-possession, the rebellious
angels had gained control of the bodies of both the sons
and daughters of the sinful men of the primeval world,
developing their progeny into evil giants who brought
great violence on the earth. Such illicit possession of the
bodies of human beings and attempted corruption of all
human flesh had finally led God to bring that great judgment on the earth in the days of Noah (Genesis 6:1-13).
The worship of the faithful angels takes place in the
beautiful temple of God in heaven ("the beauty of holiness [the sanctuary]"), immediately following God's victory over the wicked angels and their human instruments.

THE VOICE OF THE LORD (Verses 3-9)

The first two verses of the psalm are an exhortation to
praise. The remainder of the psalm contains the

response of praise, as the heavenly host recounts the judgments of the Lord in the great Flood, culminating in victory over the wicked ones.

Seven times, the "voice of the Lord" speaks, each time resulting in mighty works in the earth. It is an interesting comparison to note that, in the Genesis record of the Flood, there are exactly seven times when God spoke to Noah (Genesis 6:13; 7:1; 8:15; 9:1, 8, 12, 17). In each case, however, though the scene was one of judgment, God's word to Noah was one of grace. Likewise, in a future time of worldwide judgment, there will again be a seven-fold voice from heaven: ". . . and when he cried, seven thunders uttered their voices" (Revelation 10:3). The message of the seven thunders is evidently also one of grace in the midst of judgment, but the precise message is not yet revealed (Revelation 10:1-7).

That there is a connection Biblically between the seven thunders in Revelation and the seven voices of the Lord in Psalm 29 is indicated by the thunder accompanying the first of these:

1. "The voice of the Lord is upon the waters: the God of glory thundereth: the Lord is upon many waters" (verse 3). This was no doubt the first time the angry sound of thunder had ever echoed in God's beautiful world. There had never been a rainstorm before (Genesis 2:5), but suddenly "many waters" poured down from the heavens and up from the great deep (Genesis 7:11, 12).

2. "The voice of the Lord is powerful" (verse 4). Tremendous reservoirs of energy were unleashed as the fountains of the great deep burst open and the giant floodgates in the skies released their torrents. These energies soon would devastate and level the globe.

3. "The voice of the Lord is full of majesty" (verse 4). The Hebrew word is the same as "honour," and the testimony is one of God's reaffirmed sovereignty. Satan, through his host of fallen spirits, with a multitude of corrupt men and women whose bodies they had possessed, and the race of giants they had fathered, had filled the

earth with violent wickedness, but the longsuffering of God had finally been exhausted and the judgment had come.

4. "The voice of the Lord breaketh the cedars" (verse 5). The mighty trees of the verdant antediluvian forests (which, in his vision, could only be described by David as like the cedars of Lebanon) were broken and uprooted by the rushing waters. With the vegetation all eventually washed away in great mats, the fields and hills were bare and easily eroded. Further, the erupting fountains of the deep had been followed by tremendous earthquakes and landslides; the mountains (like David's Hermon and Sirion) were skipping like a calf and a young "unicorn" (or wild bull).

5. "The voice of the Lord divideth the flames of fire" (verse 7). The Hebrew for "divideth" is actually "digs out." The picture is one of fiery lavas and burning vapors emerging from the depths. The rocks of the earth bear abundant witness to the vast amounts of igneous rocks that were laid down during the year of the Flood.

6. "The voice of the Lord shaketh the wilderness" (verse 8). After the overwhelming waters had uprooted the forests and eroded the hills, after the great earth movements and igneous flows had restructured the earth's crust, and then after new continents had arisen from the depths and the waters had retreated into new basins (Psalm 104:8, 9), the land surfaces had become utterly barren. It was a wilderness, and David could think of no more apt comparison than to call it the desolate wilderness of Kadesh. But then, the wilderness began to *shake*! The original language is graphic, describing a female in travail, about to give birth to her young. It is the same word as "calve" in verse 9, and is often translated by "travail" or a similar term. The figure of speech depicts the barren wilderness as ready to bring forth its grass and trees again, the powerful voice of the Lord bringing new life to a dead world.

7. "The voice of the Lord maketh the hinds to calve, and discovereth the forests" (verse 9). This final word

from heaven enabled the animal population, represented only by two survivors of each kind, to multiply
rapidly to replenish the earth. Simultaneously the
quivering ground brought forth great trees once again, as
the voice of the Lord "discovereth" (literally "draws
out") the forests.

"And in His temple doth everyone speak of His glory"
(literally "answer 'glory'!"). The old world was buried
and the new world born, despite the concerted rebellion
of the legions of Satan and the world of mankind. The
mere *voice* of the Lord was greater than all! And this was
sufficient to warrant the great shout of "Glory!" from
the heavenly host.

STRENGTH FOR HIS PEOPLE
(Verses 10, 11)

Psalm 29 began with a two-verse prologue, introduc-
ing the angels of heaven, and finally concludes with a
two-verse epilogue, giving their last chorus of praise and
victory. The seven verses between record the seven-times
sounded "voice of the lord" and the global renovations
proceeding therefrom.

In the epilogue, the angelic climactic chorus sounds
forth: "The Lord sitteth upon the Flood; yea, the Lord
sitteth king forever" (verse 10). The word "sitteth"
means literally "sits still." All the violence stirred up by
men and devils could be quelled merely by God's spoken
word; He did not even need to arise from His throne!
The devastating cataclysm which destroyed the world of
the antediluvians left God still seated calmly as the eternal King. His majesty unruffled, His throne secure
against the wiles of Lucifer (Isaiah 14:12-15), the Lord
omnipotent reigneth!

And so the final verse of the psalm is a word of comfort
and encouragement to all those of His creatures who
trust Him. No matter what future attacks may be made
against God's people by man or demon, "the Lord will
give strength unto His people." Even in the future fiery

judgment of the world, God is as able to keep His people through the Fire as He was through the Flood. "The Lord will bless His people with peace."

Chapter 6

THE MIGHTY WORD
OF CREATION
(Psalm 33)

INTRODUCTION

Psalm 33 is one of only four anonymous psalms in Book I of the Psalms, the others being Psalms 1, 2, and 10. All the others (through Psalm 41) are attributed to David. Acts 4:25 attributes Psalm 2 to David, and it might seem appropriate that the First Psalm would have been David's as well. Psalm 10 seems clearly to be a continuation of Psalm 9, and Psalm 33 quite possibly ties in to Psalm 32. Also Psalm 33 is attributed to David in the Septuagint Version.

The dominant theme of the 33rd Psalm is the Word of the Lord, and it is appropriate that it contains 22 verses, corresponding to the number of letters in the Hebrew alphabet. Three tremendous statements are made concerning the Word. In verse 4, it is claimed that "the word of the Lord is right." According to verse 6, "by the word of the Lord were the heavens made." Then, in verse 9, "He spake, and it was done." God's Word, therefore, is *right* and *powerful* and *certain*!

In addition to a strong emphasis on the *Word* of God, Psalm 33 emphasizes the *works* of God. Its 22 verses divide naturally into four stanzas of four, five, six, and seven verses, respectively. Verses 1-4 contain an exhortation to praise the works of God; verses 5-9 constitute a testimony to God's work of creation, verses 10-15 a testimony to God's work of providence, and verses 16-22 a testimony to God's work of salvation.

EXHORTATION TO PRAISE GOD'S WORKS (Verses 1-4)

Verse 1 begins with a command which echoes the last verse of Psalm 32, exhorting the righteous to rejoice and praise the Lord, for praise (not boasting!) is comely for the one who has received the Lord's righteousness. The second and third verses call for praise in song, accompanied by those who can play "skillfully with a loud noise" (not just noisily!). Two musical instruments are specifically mentioned, the "harp" (probably the four-stringed lyre) and the "psaltery — an instrument of ten strings." To these today could no doubt be added the many-stringed piano, as well as other instruments (see Psalm 150).

The exhortation, furthermore, is to sing a *new* song, one with a glorious theme not before sung in the psalms. For the first time, the grand work of creation is to be extolled, giving honor to the Creator. This is the first of six "new songs" in the book of Psalms (the others in Psalm 40:3; 96:1; 98:1; 144:9; and 149:1).

The reason for such rejoicing and praise and singing is given, finally, in verse 4. "For the word of the Lord is right; and all His works are done in truth." What a testimony! "I esteem all thy precepts concerning all things to be right" (Psalm 119:128). His works are done, literally, in "steadfastness." They will stand forever because they are true. Whether or not we understand, we can have absolute confidence that whatever God says is right and whatever He does will stand, for the simple reason that He is God.

GOD'S WORK OF CREATION (Verses 5-9)

In these verses is found perhaps the strongest affirmation of fiat creation in the Bible. After an introductory acknowledgment that the entire earth manifests God's goodness (literally "mercy"), as well as the righteousness and judgment which His nature loves, the psalmist harks back to the record of its very creation, when God created it with these purposes in His heart.

Note that it was not just by the Lord, but by the *Word* of the Lord that the heavens were made. This, of course, is a reference back to the account of creation in Genesis 1, in which there are no less than 17 references to God speaking. It further anticipates the manifestation of God in and to His creation, under the name of The Word (John 1:1-3) by whom all things were made and who became flesh, as the incarnate Son of God. In the New Testament, of course, Jesus Christ is clearly recognized as the Creator (Colossians 1:16; Hebrews 1:2; Ephesians 3:9). Reference to the Word of God as the one by whom the heavens and earth were originally made is also found in II Peter 3:5.

The "heavens" constitute the space component of the space-mass-time universe, and the "host of them" include both the stars (Jeremiah 33:22) and the angels (II Chronicles 18:18), both of which are *in* the heavens. All were made by the "breath of His mouth," but this phrase might very well be translated the "spirit of His mouth," (the Hebrew *ruach* is translated either "wind," or "breath," or "spirit," depending on context), thus reflecting the work of the Spirit as described in Genesis 1:2.

Verse 7 is a reference to the "deep" of Genesis 1:2 (same word as "depth") and the "gathering together of the waters" is a reference both to the waters under and over the firmament (Genesis 1:6-8) and the gathering of the waters under the firmament into "seas" (Genesis 1:9-10). These were laid up in "storehouses," to provide the antediluvian hydrologic cycle and the wonderful climatic environment prepared originally by God for the created world. In another sense, these waters were also stored up to serve as waters of judgment in the great Flood (II Peter 3:6) when the "fountains" of this "great deep" were broken up (Genesis 7:11). It was probably in reference to this event that the psalmist in verse 7 exhorted the inhabitants of the earth to fear and stand in awe of the Lord.

Finally verse 9 says, literally, "For He spake, and it *was*; He commanded, and it *stood*." There was no process of creation, no time involved. God's Word is omnipotent, and when He speaks in creative power, the result is instantaneous. There is obviously no possibility of "evolution" in such an act of fiat creation. The entities created by God were created complete and mature and functioning right from the start. "For He commanded, and they were created. He hath also stablished them for ever and ever" (Psalm 148:5, 6).

GOD'S WORK OF PROVIDENCE
(Verses 10-15)

The next six verses of Psalm 33 stress God's overruling sovereignty in the world He had created, especially among the nations that had been established after the Flood. Though these nations had gone in their own ways, ignoring their maker, He was still in control and was working especially through His chosen nation. Verses 10 and 11 contrast the "counsel of the nations" (that is, their doctrines and philosophy) "which is brought to naught," with the "counsel of the Lord" which stands forever. The "devices of the people" will be made of no effect, but "the thoughts" (same word as "devices") of God's heart will endure to all generations. All of man's vaunted knowledge and wisdom are foolish and will come to nothing (I Corinthians 2:6, 3:19), and it is therefore futile for us to spend years being educated in this wisdom rather than in the true wisdom of God according to the Scriptures.

Verses 12-15 give assurance that God indeed is in control. He "beholds all," according to verse 13; He "fashions all" and "understands all" in verse 15. He is thus omnipresent, omnipotent, and omniscient. In sovereign grace, therefore, He "chooses" His own (verse 12). Even though He chose a particular nation, however, He still deals with all the nations. The Noahic covenant (Genesis 9:6, 9) is still in effect (Romans 13:1; Acts 17:26), and God still rules the nations through His divinely established institution of human government.

GOD'S WORK OF SALVATION
(Verses 16-22)

The final section of Psalm 33 extols the third of God's great works, that of salvation, or deliverance. First, the psalmist in verses 16 and 17 stresses that real salvation cannot be found in those things to which most men look. It is not to be found in the "multitude of an host," that is, not by *military power*. Neither is it in "much strength," or *manpower*. Also, a horse is "a vain thing for safety" (literally, "salvation"), so it is not in *horsepower*.

Salvation is only in the Lord and *His* power! "The eye of the Lord is upon them that fear Him" (verse 18). The "eyes of the Lord" symbolize the care and protection of the Lord. They are "upon the righteous" (Psalm 34:15), and they "preserve knowledge" (Proverbs 22:12). They are "in every place, beholding the evil and the good" (Proverbs 15:3); and "all the goings" of man (Proverbs 5:21). They "run to and fro throughout the whole earth, to shew Himself strong in the behalf of them whose heart is perfect toward Him" (II Chronicles 16:9).

God's great deliverance is received by those who "hope in His mercy" — that is, who believe in His grace. To these, He supplies all the material needs of life (verse 19), as well as guidance ("help") and protection ("shield") to those who "wait for the Lord" (verse 20). Furthermore, true joy in salvation is shared by all who trust in His name (verse 21).

In verse 5, it was noted that the entire earth, as created, was "full of the goodness of the Lord." The word "goodness" is the same word as "mercy" in verses 18 and 22, often translated "loving-kindness." The "goodness" with which the beautiful earth was clothed when God pronounced it "very good" (Genesis 1:31) is also "upon us, according as we hope in thee." That "hope" (verses 18, 22) is merely confident faith in God's Word. And since the Word of the Lord is right and powerful and sure, our hope in Him is secure forever!

Chapter 7

THE DAYS OF OUR YEARS
(Psalm 90)

The 90th Psalm is probably the oldest of all the psalms. According to the Received Text, David is recognized as author of 75 of the psalms, Asaph as author of 12, and Ethan of one. No definite author is listed for 60 of them, although it is probable that David wrote many of these. This 90th Psalm, however, is ascribed to Moses, the man of God (because of similarity in phraseology, it is quite possible that Moses also wrote Psalm 91). It is placed as the opening chapter in Book IV of the Psalms (the Book of Psalms is divided into five Books, beginning with Psalms 1, 42, 73, 90, and 107, respectively).

THE EVERLASTING GOD
(Verses 1-4)

The setting seems to be at the entrance to the promised land toward the very end of Moses' life. The end of his writings had been "the blessing wherewith Moses the man of God blessed the children of Israel before his death" (Deuteronomy 33:1). Then, perhaps, followed this psalm, "a prayer of Moses the man of God" (Psalm 90, superscript). Moses had studied the records of all the patriarchs, from Adam through Jacob, and had edited and recorded them in final form in the Book of Genesis, and no doubt they had made a profound impression on him. Then he had recorded all of God's dealings with himself and the children of Israel, both in Egypt and in the wilderness, and he was keenly aware of the unity and comprehensiveness of God's plan in history for mankind everywhere in all ages. It is this big picture which dominates the 90th Psalm.

And what a picture! Wherever God was, that's where home was! Whether in the Garden of Eden, in the violent world of the antediluvians, in the Ark during the great Flood, in a tent in the land of Canaan, in bondage in Egypt or following the Cloud in the wilderness, Jehovah Himself had always been their abiding place. In this life, the people of God are pilgrims and have no certain dwelling place, for they seek a city with foundations, whose builder and maker is God (Hebrews 11:8-14).

Moses, recalling how God had "formed the earth and the world" (that is, the basic elements of the ground and also the beautiful inhabitable cosmos made from those elements), stressed that God existed prior to all creation. Only in the Bible do we find such a revelation of God's eternal preexistence. All other religious "scriptures" begin with eternal matter in some form, and thus do not attempt to explain real *creation*. The true God, however, was before all things. The Creator, of course, is none other than Christ Himself — the "Alpha and Omega" (Revelation 1:8).

After the Creation came the Fall, and then the Curse. Moses recalls this sad event as well: "Thou turnest man to destruction [literally 'crumbling' — that is, the 'dust' of Genesis 3:19]; and sayest, Return, ye children of men [or, literally, 'Adam']." Though God had formed all things, even the human body, from the dust of the earth, they would all eventually return back to the dust. This principle of "crumbling" is now known to be so universally true, as to be recognized scientifically as the *law* of increasing entropy, or disorder, one of the two basic laws of science.

For a long time after the Curse, however, men continued to live almost a thousand years before dying. The average age of the antediluvian patriarchs (excluding

Enoch, who did not die at all) was 912 years, and one of them (Methuselah) lived 969 years. But their days had been almost forgotten by the time of Moses' generation. Even a man who could live a thousand years would be forgotten soon after he was gone. And in God's sight, such a tremendous span of time (as humans measure time) would be trivial indeed.

Life-spans had greatly deteriorated after the Flood, so that Moses, at age 120 years, was 60 years older than any of his contemporaries. All of those who would have been older than 60 years of age had died in the wilderness (see Numbers 14:29, 34; Deuteronomy 34:7). Because of all this, Moses was profoundly impressed with the ephemeral nature of human longevity in contrast to God's timelessness.

Men today casually discuss geological dates in terms of millions and billions of years, but this is mere evolutionary vacuity. Such dates are meaningless in terms of man's experience. He can barely recall events of his own earlier years, and historical data of only two millennia ago are regarded as *ancient* history. The human mind cannot begin to comprehend the concept of a million or a billion years.

This verse (Psalm 90:4) has often been combined with II Peter 3:8 by modern commentators, and then both used to justify the notion that the six days of creation in Genesis correspond to the evolutionary ages of geology. Such strained exegesis is contradicted by the contexts of both verses, and there is no good evidence that Peter was even referring to Moses' statement at all. In Psalm 90, Moses is contrasting the brevity of man's life — even those antediluvian men who lived almost a thousand years — with the changeless and ageless Creator.

FINITE, MORTAL MAN
(Verses 5-11)

This contrast is further stressed in the next section of the psalm. The span of human life is first likened to the debris carried away by a flood (probably the antediluvians carried off by the great Noahic Deluge, along with the massive plant and animal remains now preserved as fossils in the sedimentary rocks), then to a dream in a single night's sleep, and then to the grass that grows and soon withers. Indeed, "all flesh is like grass" (Isaiah 40:6-8; I Peter 1:24; Psalm 103:14, 16), ever since the Curse came on the world.

The problem is not biological, but theological. Gerontologists will never reverse the process of aging and death by scientific research, though they may be able to retard it slightly. As long as there is sin, there will be death, "for we are consumed by thine anger." There are two aspects to sin, "iniquities" — that is, overt acts of sin — and "secret sins" — that is the sin-nature which impels us to sin even when we are not consciously sinning. Both aspects are exposed "in the light of thy countenance."

Every babe entering the world inherits such a nature, and thus "*all* our days" are spent in the presence of God's wrath. Consequently, in contrast to God's unending life and to His original purpose for man's life, "we spend our years as a sigh." In the Authorized Version, the rendering is "tale that is told," but the word is, simply, "sigh," very brief and conscious of futility. As James says: "for what is your life? It is even a vapour, that appeareth for a little time, and then vanisheth away" (James 4:14). As Paul says: "God hath made the creation subject to vanity [that is, 'futility'] " (Romans 8:20).

Then, in the midst of these melancholy thoughts, Moses pens his classic lament: "The days of our years are threescore years and ten." Though Moses himself was 120 years old, and though he had been contemplating the golden age of the past when men lived a thousand years, all others of his own people were only 60 years of age, or younger, and he knew the normal lifespan could never again greatly exceed 70 years, as long as the present world order prevailed. Under some conditions, men might live to 80 years of age or a little older, but such old age would involve little but "labour and sorrow," exactly as God had told Adam himself (Genesis 3:17, 19). Very soon, at best, the body would be "cut off," and the spirit would "fly away."

Men fear growing old and dying, and do all they can to avoid or delay it, often complaining against God because of it, forgetting that it all results from God's curse on sin. The great power of God's wrath and anger, though not recognized or understood by lost men, is ample reason to fear the Lord, and men should be instructed by the very fact of the mysterious and unnatural brevity of their own lives to seek God's forgiveness and guidance.

TRUE WISDOM AND SALVATION
(Verses 12-17)

The remaining verses of Psalm 90 constitute a prayer for God's complete salvation. Man is helpless and dying, but God is mighty and eternal. Only He can grant true wisdom and endless life. Since our days are few, and since even those few days are passed in the presence of God's wrath and are full of labor and sorrow, we need to "number our days, in order to acquire a heart of wisdom."

As already acknowledged, the number of the days of man's years corresponds only to seventy years, and probably not more than fifty years (18,000 days) of these can be used for productive work for God. How urgent, therefore, to use each of these days effectively. "O that they were wise, that they understood this, that they would consider their latter end!" (Deuteronomy 32:29). "See then that ye walk circumspectly, not as fools, but as wise, redeeming the time, because the days are evil" (Ephesians 5:15, 16).

True wisdom is found only in God, Himself, as well as true salvation from life's futility. "But of Him are ye in Christ Jesus, who of God is made unto us wisdom, and

righteousness, and sanctification, and redemption"
(I Corinthians 1:30).

At the time God pronounced the Curse, He also made
the first promise of a coming Savior who would make all
things right again (Genesis 3:15).

But the ages have passed, and the Curse seems more
bitter than ever. Moses cries out: "How long, O Lord?"
The promise had seemed long delayed even to Moses. In
our day, the promised deliverance from the Curse has
been delayed yet another 3000 years, but the Apostle
Peter reminds us that "the long-suffering of our Lord is
salvation" (II Peter 3:15).

Moses climaxes his prayer with seven specific requests
to the Lord, which we could well make our own in these
latter days:

1. *"Let it repent thee concerning thy servants."* As
Paul says: "the earnest expectation of the creation is
waiting for the manifestation of the sons of God . . . . we
ourselves groan within ourselves, waiting for the adop-
tion, to wit, the redemption of our body" (Romans 8:19,
23).

2. *"O satisfy us early* [i.e., 'in the morning'] *with thy
mercy; that we may rejoice and be glad all our days."*
Salvation and true happiness are gifts of God's grace,
but those who receive it early may pass all their days —
even though man's days are days of sorrow under God's
curse — as days of joy, "as sorrowful, yet always rejoicing" (II Corinthians 6:10).

3. *"Make us glad according to the days wherein thou
hast afflicted us, and the years wherein we have seen
evil."* In verse 4 ("a thousand years are as yesterday"),
verse 9 ("our days are passed away in thy wrath . . . . our
years as a sigh"), and verse 10 ("the days of our
years . . . . are labor and sorrow"), man's days and years
are brought together. Days stretch into years and years
into thousands of years, and yet God still delays. Some
day, however, He *will* come and "our light affliction,
which is but for a moment, worketh for us a far more ex-

ceeding and eternal weight of glory" (II Corinthians
4:17).

4. *"Let thy work appear unto thy servants."* If only we
could understand the world and man as God sees them,
what a transformation it would make in our lives. Indeed, his servants, redeemed from sin, themselves
constitute the greatest of the mighty works of God
(Ephesians 2:10).

5. *"And thy glory unto their children."* Even more
important than to understand the work of God is to comprehend the glory of God. When we see Him as He is, we
shall finally become *like* He is (I John 3:2).

6. *"Let the beauty of the Lord our God* [i.e., 'Jehovah
our Elohim'] *be upon us."* When His "workmanship"
(literally, His "poem," His great masterwork (Ephesians
2:10) is complete in us, we — like His completed physical creation — will be "very good" (Genesis 1:31). All
three of the great names of God appear in this psalm —
Adonai (verse 1), *Elohim* (verse 2), *Jehovah* (verse 3),
and then *Jehovah our Elohim* in the final verse. As all
the fullness of God dwells bodily in Christ (Colossians
2:9), so all His love and beauty shall become ours
through Christ.

7. *"And establish thou the work of our hands upon
us."* In this life it is vital, first that we recognize *God's*
work (verse 16) and, then, that He order and establish
our work. It must be in this order, of course. "Work out
your own salvation with fear and trembling. For it is God
which worketh in you both to will and to do of His good
pleasure" (Philippians 2:12, 13).

Therefore, although we must in this present age live
under the Curse, with its bondage to sin and death, we
can — like Moses — look by faith into the promised land
across the Jordan and thereby live by faith victoriously
even in this present world.

Chapter 8

ANGELS AND DRAGONS
(Psalm 91)

BACKGROUND

The 91st Psalm is certainly one of the mountain-peak chapters of the Bible, speaking to both heart and mind and assuring the godly believer of God's blessing and protection under all circumstances. Not even the fiery dragon can prevail against God's mighty angels! Psalm 91 has the unique distinction of having been quoted (really misquoted!) by none other than Satan himself when he was tempting Christ, suggesting that this is really a section of Scripture that gives Satan intense concern and which he would like most to destroy if possible.

No author is listed for this psalm, but it is at least plausible that it may originally have come from Moses. The preceding psalm (90) has always been attributed to Moses, and there are certain common themes and terms in the two psalms, as well as indications that the miraculous deliverance of the Israelites from Egypt was in the mind of the writer as he wrote.

The first verse of Psalm 90, for example, speaks of the Lord as our "dwelling place." The same Hebrew word is used in Psalm 91:10, speaking of making the Lord our "habitation." The brevity of human life is stressed in Psalm 90, and then Psalm 91 assures the trusting believer "long life," probably meaning eternal life. The

references to deliverance from armies and plagues in
Psalm 91 are most understandable in light of God's
power as shown against the Egyptians. Although it is
not possible to say for certain that Moses wrote the
psalm, it at least makes it beautifully understandable
to regard it as Moses' own *personal* testimony,
supplementing his psalm for the nation as a whole, so to
speak, in Psalm 90. Even if this is true, of course, it can
likewise be appropriated as the personal experience and
testimony of any believer.

INVITATION TO TRUST THE LORD
(Verse 1)

Psalm 91 seems to be divided into four main sections,
as follows:

1. Verse One is an invitation and testimony from a
    Witness, perhaps the Holy Spirit Himself, spoken
    in the third person, offering God's salvation to
    that one who will trust Him.
2. Verse Two is the acceptance of that invitation and
    a statement of faith by the responding believer
    (Moses originally, perhaps).
3. Verses 3 through 13, the bulk of the psalm, is the
    testimony of assurance and guidance given to the
    new convert, again by the divine witness in the
    third person.
4. Verses 14 through 16 is a confirming promise from
    God Himself, given in the first person directly to
    the believer, assuring Him of the validity of the
    great promises made by the Witness in verses 1
    and 3-13, and then extending them even more.

The first section, consisting of one verse only, is a
beautiful promise which draws the listener directly to
the heart of God. "He that sits down [literal meaning of
'dwelleth' here] in the secret place of the most High
[Hebrew *Elyon*] shall pass the night under the shadow of
the Almighty [Hebrew *Shaddai*]." God is introduced
under two of His less-used names, both of which stress

His ability to protect and sustain the believer. The "Most High" is *over* all; the "Almighty" is *under* all, providing sustenance and support (the word *Shaddai* is derived from the Hebrew *shad*, meaning "breast").

The "secret place" is actually the "hiding place." The picture is of one finding rest and protection and nourishment in God's bosom like a helpless child, during the dark and dangerous night of life in a world under Satan's control. It is the same word as in Psalm 119:114: "Thou art my hiding place and my shield." Therefore, as the Apostle says, "Set your affection on things above, not on things on the earth. For ye are dead, and your life is hid with Christ in God" (Colossians 3:2, 3).

ACCEPTANCE OF THE LORD
(Verse 2)

Such a wonderful promise should certainly not be refused. Accordingly, the believer does respond, accepting the gracious invitation: "I will say of the Lord [Hebrew *Jehovah*], He is my refuge and my fortress: my God [Hebrew *Elohim*]; in Him will I trust."

Two little-used names of God were used in the first verse, but the two *most*-used names appear in this second verse. God is all and in all, and it takes many names to adequately describe His attributes, many figures of speech to describe His relation to the believer. The figure of the refuge and fortress would certainly be meaningful to Moses. In his last word to the tribes, he had told them: "The eternal God is thy refuge, and underneath are the everlasting arms" (Deuteronomy 33:27). Though neither the children of Israel in the wilderness nor the Christian pilgrim in this age could ever dwell securely in a literal fortress, the Lord Himself surrounds them, that "we might have a strong consolation, who have fled for refuge to lay hold upon the hope set before us: which hope we have as an anchor of the soul, both sure and steadfast" (Hebrews 6:18, 19).

With such promises as surety, the seeking soul can sit down in confident faith. "In Him will I trust!"

THE PROMISE OF DIVINE PROTECTION
(Verses 3-13)

Again the divine Witness speaks, giving assurance of all needed protection and guidance to the new believer, in verses 3 through 13. The figures seem often directly taken from the actual experiences of Moses and the children of Israel in Egypt and the wilderness, where they were not symbols at all, but real dangers!

They had been like helpless chicks, but He had said: "Ye have seen what I did to the Egyptians, and how I bare you on eagles' wings, and brought you to myself" (Exodus 19:4). Note also Deuteronomy 32:9-13; etc. So He promises: "He shall deliver thee from the snare of the fowler and the deadly pestilence." He also had said to Moses: "If thou wilt . . . keep all His statutes, I will put none of these diseases upon thee, which I have brought upon the Egyptians; for I am the Lord that healeth thee" (Exodus 15:26).

Continuing with the figure of the great eagle, "He shall cover thee with His feathers, and under His wings shalt thou trust." But then appears an important clarification. This is no mere sentimentalism, as is true of so much "deeper-life" teaching. "His *truth* shall be thy shield and buckler!" This implies that Satan's *lies* will be his greatest weapons against the believer. He is the great Deceiver, and his primeval humanistic lie persuading man to think he is able to play God is still his most effective tool.

But God's promises are inscripturated promises, and it is the written Word that still provides the Christian's defense, just as it was when Christ Himself defeated Satan who had misquoted this very psalm (see below). "I have given them thy word," Jesus said. "Sanctify them through thy word: thy word is truth" (John 17:14, 17). "Stand therefore, having your loins girt about with truth; . . . . Above all, taking the shield of faith, wherewith ye shall be able to quench all the fiery darts of the wicked" (Ephesians 6:14, 16).

In verse 5 is promised courage both day and night, against the daytime arrows of the enemy and the unknown dangers of the night. To the children of Israel, "the Lord went before them by day in a pillar of a cloud, to lead them the way, and by night in a pillar of fire, to give them light: to go by day and night" (Exodus 13:21). Neither midnight pestilence nor noonday attack could harm them (verse 6). "A thousand shall fall at thy side, and ten thousand at thy right hand; but it shall not come nigh thee." The armies of Moses had experienced this very thing in reverse when they had rebelled against God. "How should one chase a thousand, and two put ten thousand to flight, except their Rock had sold them, and the Lord had shut them up?" (Deuteronomy 32:30). But God is an impregnable refuge and fortress to His trusting ones!

"Only with thine eye shalt thou behold and see the reward of the wicked" (verse 8). This also had been their experience. "And Moses said unto the people, Fear ye not, stand still, and see the salvation of the Lord . . . . And Israel saw that great work which the Lord did upon the Egyptians: and the people feared the Lord" (Exodus 14:13, 31). "And to you who are troubled, rest with us, when the Lord Jesus shall be revealed from heaven with His mighty angels; In flaming fire taking vengeance on them that know not God, and that obey not the gospel of our Lord Jesus Christ" (II Thessalonians 1:7, 8). The mighty plagues and miracles by which God routed the ancient Egyptians are firmly anchored as facts of history, regardless of the skepticism of modern scientists. The very existence of Israel is proof of God's power to preserve His own.

In verse 9, there is a brief parenthesis, reminding the believer again just *why* God will bless him so. "Because thou hast made [referring back to his confession of faith in verse 2] the Lord 'My refuge' [quoting what he had said], the most High thy dwelling place." How infinite are the resources of him who truly trusts God!

Continuing his assurances, the Witness promises: "There shall no evil befall thee, neither shall any plague come nigh thy dwelling." Because, of course, that dwelling-place is God Himself! In Egypt, during the awful plagues on the Egyptians, neither the flies, nor the murrain, nor the boils, nor the hail, nor the thick darkness, nor the death angel, entered the dwellings or fields of the children of Israel (Exodus 8:22; 9:6, 11, 26; 10:23; 11:7).

But how is it that the Lord places such marvelous protection around His people? It is through His mighty angels!

"For He shall give His angels charge over thee, to keep thee in all thy ways. They shall bear thee up in their hands, lest thou dash thy foot against a stone" (verses 11, 12).

There does exist an "innumerable company of angels" (Hebrews 12:22), that "excel in strength" (Psalm 103:20), whose very purpose is "to minister for them who shall be heirs of salvation" (Hebrews 1:14). "The angel of the Lord encampeth round about them that fear Him, and delivereth them" (Psalm 34:7).

There is no ground for presumption in all these glorious promises, of course. Such angelic protection is conditioned on our making the Most High our habitation and making His truth our shield and buckler. There is no safer place in the cosmos than in the center of God's will, as recognized through faith in His Word, but there is darkness and pestilence and fearfulness outside.

And when it is time for the believer finally to enter into the light of God's personal presence (not just the *shadow* of the Almighty!) then these very angels will accompany him through the valley of death and translate him in his spiritual body through the heavens to Christ's throne (Luke 16:22; II Corinthians 5:8).

These verses (Psalm 91:11, 12) are the verses which Satan used unsuccessfully in trying to persuade Christ to cast himself down from the pinnacle of the temple

(Matthew 4:5-7; Luke 4:9-12). But the great deceiver, true to his character, misquoted and distorted God's words, just as he had done long before with Eve. This time, he omitted the key words "*in all thy ways*." Angels would indeed keep Him in all *His* ways, but Christ's ways were not Satan's ways! His answer; "Thou shalt not tempt the Lord thy God," shows that faith in God's promise is no ground for presumption and boastful display.

So will angels today "keep" us in all our ways, but these ways must please the Lord. "In all thy ways acknowledge Him, and He shall direct thy paths" (Proverbs 3:6).

The next verse (13) climaxes this section, and indicates why Satan desired so urgently to destroy Christ with his temptation. "Thou shalt tread upon the lion and adder: the young lion and dragon shalt thou trample under feet." This also is a promise for protection against the most dangerous animals, even dragons. This word (Hebrew *tannin*) actually means "dragon," not "snake," as is evident from its other occurrences. It most likely refers to some extinct reptile such as the dinosaur, which had no doubt survived the Flood long enough to be well known to the ancient world. Other references to dragons in the Bible, as well as to the *behemoth* and *leviathan* (see, especially, Job 40, 41), together with recent discoveries of fossilized human and dinosaur footprints in the same rock formations, as well as of dinosaur pictographs made by early tribesmen, all confirm the implication (evolutionists' claims notwithstanding) that men and dinosaurs once lived contemporaneously.

In any case, the terminology here evidently goes beyond the actual trampling and slaying of lions and reptilian monsters. Genesis 3:15, the great promise of a future crushing of Satan, that old serpent, by the "seed of the woman," was probably in Moses' mind as he penned these words. These are perhaps among Moses' last words, just as Genesis was the first book he had compiled and recorded, and such a thought would be

most appropriate at this point. Not only would the Lord
protect his people against all their enemies, He would
eventually destroy the greatest enemy of all — that old
Serpent, the roaring Lion, the great Dragon, the one who
had opposed God and His plan through the ages. And in
anticipation of that great victory, we can, through His
power, defeat the enemy in his temporal attacks against
us even now. "And the God of peace shall bruise Satan
under your feet shortly" (Romans 16:20).

GOD'S PERSONAL ASSURANCE
(Verses 14-16)

In the final section of this great psalm, verses 14-16,
God speaks directly to the believer, confirming the
promises of the Witness in the preceding verses. This is
the explicit answer to the believer's confession of faith in
verse 2.

"Because he hath set his love upon me, therefore will I
deliver him; I will set him on high, because he hath
known my name." Deliverance in response to real love
— exaltation because of true knowledge! Moses had
good reason to recognize the value of knowing God's holy
name, because he had been introduced to Him under
never-to-be-forgotten circumstances in the wilderness
(Exodus 3:14, 15).

Thus, not only does God assure the believer of physical deliverance, as had already been promised by the
Witness, but of glorification in heaven! In verse 15, He
makes four more amazing promises: (1) the promise of
answered prayer; (2) the promise of the presence of God
himself, not of the protecting angels alone; (3) the
promise to arm him, evidently with divine armor (this is
a better translation than "deliver"; in the King James
Version, there are three different Hebrew words all translated "deliver" in this psalm, in verses 3, 14, and 15);
(4) the promise finally to *honour* him. It is a testimony of
amazing grace that the God of all holiness should *save* a

sinner, but that He should even *honour* him is yet more amazing!

In the very last verse is the climax of all that has gone before. "With long life will I satisfy him." The phrase "long life" is really "length of days," and the context indicates the meaning really to be "forever." It is in fact, so translated in Psalm 23:6 — "I will dwell in the house of the Lord forever." The believer is promised everlasting life as the satisfaction of his trust in God. Then, lastly, "I will show him my salvation." God's great salvation for lost men has cost the shed blood of His own Son, so it is infinitely great, and He will show it to us in eternity. "That in the ages to come, He might show the exceeding riches of His grace in His kindness toward us through Christ Jesus" (Ephesians 2:7).

Chapter 9

EARTH'S PRIMEVAL AGES (Psalm 104)

The 104th Psalm is one of the most important chapters in the Bible dealing with the early history of the world. It first sets forth some of the amazing truths concerning the very first events of creation week, then discusses the gap in history caused by the great Flood, and finally the events establishing the post-flood world.

THE BEGINNING OF CREATION
(Verses 1-3)

The Psalm opens with the same exhortation with which the previous psalm had closed: "Bless the Lord, O my soul." As the writer — presumably David, who had also written Psalm 103 — began to catch a glimpse of the magnificent vision God was about to give him, He had to break out in an excited exclamation of praise, "O Lord my God, thou art very great; thou art clothed with honour and majesty." The glory of God was breaking in on his soul just as it had broken in on the universe in the beginning of the creation.

Now the very first thing that happened in this created universe was the entrance of God Himself into it, in the very act of creating it. This is the testimony of verse 2: "Who coverest [literally 'arrayest'] thyself with light as with a garment." He had been from eternity covered

with honor and majesty, but now also clothed Himself with
the actual physical light which He created.

God, ever since, has been "dwelling in the light which no
man can approach unto" (I Timothy 6:16). The basic
energy of matter and all phenomena in the physical universe is light energy. Indeed, "God is light" (I John 1:5).
Associated with God's light, radiating out from His presence in space and time, were the very space and time
("heaven" and "beginning") which He concurrently
created (Genesis 1:1). He "stretchest out the heavens like a
curtain." Verse 3 then alludes to the construction of God's
actual "dwelling" in these heavens. Somewhere — no man
knows where — is an actual location in the universe where
God dwells in light. It is "far above all heavens" (Ephesians 4:10) — beyond the atmospheric and sidereal
heavens, but nevertheless somewhere in the universal
"heaven," or "space," and it is there that God's essential
glory is centered.

According to this passage, there are actual "chambers"
(literally "upper chambers") erected upon "beams," all
surrounded by mighty "waters." Furthermore, it is said
that God rides upon a heavenly "chariot" composed of
great clouds, probably clouds of intense glory, and that He
"rides on the wings" of the wind (or perhaps, the "Spirit,"
since "wind" and "spirit" are both translations of the
Hebrew *ruach*).

The obvious question is whether these beams and chambers and waters and clouds are meant to be understood in
their literal sense or, if not, exactly what they do symbolize. Similar figures are used to describe the environs of
God's presence in other parts of Scripture (Ezekiel 1:4, 24;
Revelation 22:1; etc.).

A cardinal rule in Bible hermeneutics is to take any
passage primarily in the sense intended by the writer (both
human and divine), as determined from both its immediate context and the context of other related parts of
Scripture. Normally a passage would be taken literally
unless a literal sense is not possible. When figures are used,
it should be expected that the meaning of the figures is

clarified elsewhere, since the purpose of the writer is communication, not confusion.

Since no explanation is offered here, we should conclude either that the description is literal or else that the
reality of the scene is so indescribable that man can only
comprehend it in terms of an actual throne room where
God dwells in His glory. In any case, the message clearly
comes through that God's presence occupies a specific
location somewhere in His created universe. The Lord
Jesus Christ, at His ascension, was in a literal body when a
literal "cloud" received Him in sight of His disciples, and
he then ascended on into the distant heaven of God's
dwelling where He "sat down" on the right hand of the
Father (Mark 16:19; Colossians 3:1; etc.).

On the other hand, the fact that God does have an upper
chamber in the heavens where His presence is centered,
does not contradict the even greater fact of His omnipresence. Thus, in another sense, the entire cosmos is
His dwelling-place, and His glory can be especially illustrated to man in the heavens stretching over the earth
like a curtain, arrayed in light diffused around it from the
sun and stars and acting through the waters and winds and
fires that sustain life on the earth.

CREATION OF THE ANGELS
(Verses 4, 5)

According to the record here in Psalm 104, the next act
after the creation of the space-time cosmos and the es-
tablishment of God's light-arrayed throne therein was the
creation of the angels. "He maketh His angels spirits, and
His ministers a flame of fire."

Some writers, knowing that the word "angel" means
"messenger" in the Hebrew and "spirit" is the same as
"wind," have rendered this passage somewhat as follows:
"He makes the wind his messenger and the fire his servant." This cannot be the full meaning, however, since the
New Testament quotes this verse in such a way that it
could only mean *angels* (see Hebrews 1:7). Angels

are mighty spirit-beings, and they were evidently created right at this time.

This remarkable verse seems also to state that these servants of God are actually also composed of flaming fire, in addition to being spirits. This concept is beyond our naturalistic comprehension, but that is no reason for us to reject or spiritualize it prematurely. We do not know the nature of angels. Man was made of the natural chemical elements ("dust of the earth") and is, therefore, subject to the electromagnetic and gravitational forces which control these elements. Angels have the remarkable ability to assume the *appearance* of men, including the actual biological and material substance (note Genesis 18:8), but they are normally invisible spirits, though quite real. They can "fly swiftly" (Daniel 9:21) from God's throne to earth when so commanded and are not limited by gravity or other natural forces. They are often in Scripture associated directly with the stars of heaven — which, of course, are orbs of flaming fire, — and it may be that the essential structure of their "bodies" is analogous to that of the stars. In any case, they are often closely associated in the Bible with an appearance of fire (Genesis 3:24; II Thessalonians 1:7, 8; etc.).

People often think that angels must have existed in some fourth dimensional state long before this present world was made. Indeed, they were certainly present before the earth received its *foundations*. Angels are seen as singing together and shouting for joy when God laid the earth's foundations (Job 38:4-7). Also, here in Psalm 104, verse 5 speaks of God laying the foundations of the earth, right after He made the angels in verse 4 (in this verse, however, a better translation might be "He established the habitation of the earth" — that is, its position as a distinct body in space).

On the other hand, the basic stuff of the physical space-mass-time cosmos must have been made before God made the angels, since angels exist in the cosmos. Furthermore, they were created specifically to minister to people (Hebrews 1:14), and people live in the cosmos.

The "earth" of Genesis 1:1 was originally "without form" (Genesis 1:2), so that it did not assume a definite shape or location until the Spirit of God began to "move in the presence of the waters." As the earth became spherical (as the force of gravity was activated) and energized when God called for "light," as recorded in Genesis 1:3 (and the electromagnetic force system began to function), it was still essentially a vast solution or suspension of elements in a mighty matrix of waters (note II Peter 3:5). Not until the third day, did solid earth material begin to appear in and above the waters. It is probably this series of divine acts that are referred to as "laying the foundations of the earth."

In any case, it is important to note that this foundation (or habitation) of the earth will not be removed forever. God had an eternal purpose for the earth when He created it, and though it would have to undergo a mighty cataclysm of water one day, and eventually an even greater cataclysm of fire (II Peter 3:10), it would be renewed in each case. Eventually God Himself would establish His eternal dwelling place on the renewed and perfected earth (Revelation 21:1-3).

THE COMING OF THE DELUGE
(Verses 6-9)

Verses 6 through 9 of Psalm 104 obviously refer to the great Deluge. Not until the very end of the psalm, however, is mention made of the effect of sin on the earth. The primary purpose of this psalm is simply to describe the mighty creative and providential acts of God in relation to the earth. Therefore, the narrative jumps directly from the act which called the earth out of the water to that which again plunged it beneath the waters.

"Thou coverest it with the deep as with a garment." This statement notes the contrast between God covering (literally "arraying" Himself with light as with a garment) and His covering (literally "hiding" — a different Hebrew word) the earth as with a garment. One was for display of glory, the other for covering the shame.

"The waters stood above the mountains" (see Genesis 7:19, 20), so the whole earth was inundated. The mountains so mentioned were the gentle mountains of the antediluvian topography; the next verse describes the uplift of the great and rugged mountains of the present world.

Verse 8 speaks of a gigantic earth movement which terminated the universal Flood. The eruption of the "fountains of the great deep" and the pouring of huge torrents of rain on the earth from "the windows of heaven" (Genesis 7:11) had left great empty caverns in the earth's crust and piled tremendous beds of sediments in all the antediluvian seas, leaving the crust in a state of complex stress. Eventually, great faults and earth movements began to develop. The American Standard Version renders this verse accurately as follows: "The mountains rose, the valleys sank down." Great continental uplifts took place, with corresponding sinking of the basins. A great storm of wind (Genesis 8:1) and lightning and thunder (verse 7), none of which had ever been experienced by the earth before the Flood, triggered the mighty orogenies.

Verse 9 then refers to God's promise to Noah never again to send the Flood to destroy the earth (Genesis 9:11). Job 26:10 also refers to this promise: "He hath compassed the waters with bounds, until the day and night come to an end." The isostatic equilibrium is now sufficiently established so that the sea bed can never rise again sufficiently to plunge waters over the mountains. Also, the waters remaining in the heavens and below the ground are no longer present in such quantities as to make possible a worldwide Flood.

THE WORLD AFTER THE FLOOD
(Verses 10-13)

The last part of the 104th Psalm describes God's providential arrangements for the animals and men in the vastly-changed post-Flood world. Verses 10-15 speak of His provision of food and drink; verses 16-18 tell of His arrangements for dwelling-places; verses 19-23 describe His plans for their activities; verses 24-30 summarize His universal, providential care of all His creatures; and verses 31-35 constitute a statement of the divine purpose in creation and providence, with man's acceptable response in praise.

The immediate need after the Flood, for both men and animals, was survival. The world had been literally devastated by the great cataclysm and now would have to be repopulated under much harsher environmental conditions than had prevailed in the original creation. The first need was for a new water supply system. The waters of the Flood were laden with debris and all kinds of sediments and dissolved chemicals, not to mention carcasses of dead animals and people drowned in the Flood.

The deposited sands and muds, however, formed ideal filtration systems for purifying the waters. Accordingly, although most of the waters flowed into the newly-formed ocean basins, scouring out drainage-ways and even canyons in the process, many of the waters percolated into the ground to form great subterranean waterways, from which at intervals they emerged as springs of pure water, thence forming permanent rivers in the new valleys. This provision is summarized in verse 10: "He sendeth the springs into the valleys, which run among the hills."

From the network of streams, "every beast of the field" would receive drink. Trees would thrive by them, in which the birds could live. The water table sustaining the streams would likewise support a covering of grasses and herbs, providing food both for the cattle and for man himself, who would once again be able to till the ground and raise his crops.

Once the waters of the Flood had drained into these underground aquifers, however, they would have to be maintained.

The antediluvian hydrologic cycle was evidently subterranean in nature, but the eruption of the fountains of the great deep had destroyed this mechanism. A new system would have to be instituted to water the earth and this would have to be an atmospheric mechanism. "He watereth the hills from His [upper] chambers: the earth is satisfied with the fruit of thy works" (verse 13). There had been no rain in the primeval economy (Genesis 2:5) because of the worldwide equable warm temperatures maintained by the "waters above the firmament," but these were all precipitated at the Flood. With worldwide temperature differentials now established, soon the present global atmospheric circulation was functioning and the remarkable atmospheric heat engine and water cycle were operating.

PROVISION OF FOOD AND SHELTER
(Verses 14-28)

Not only did the underground water table, the springs and rivers, and the intermittent rains make the lands green again, but they produced luscious fruits (symbolized by the vine and olive tree, producing fresh wine and oil) for man's happiness and corn and wheat to produce bread for man's strength. God was also concerned about the animals. They had been preserved on Noah's Ark and were even included in the post-Flood Noahic covenant (Genesis 9:9, 10).

There is no doubt that God cares for all His creatures; not even a bird dies without His notice, according to the Lord Jesus (Matthew 10:29). Verses 16 through 23 of this psalm describe specifically God's provision for habitation and occupation of the animals after the Flood.

First, there is mention of the growth of mighty forests, where the birds could dwell, then of high mountains and rocky terrains for certain animals which might otherwise be defenseless. Neither of these environments was suitable for human dwellings.

The day-night cycle established at creation had not been affected by the Flood, as the sun and moon continued their appointed functions relative to the earth. God had made a specific promise to Noah after the Flood that this would be so as long as the earth endured (Genesis 8:22). Man would labor to produce his own food during the day, while the carnivorous animals were resting in their lairs. The beasts of the forests, in turn, would go forth to seek their own prey at night. These are obviously general provisions, rather than inviolable laws.

The reference in verse 21 to lions seeking prey and God providing it for them indicates that the Edenic provision of only the "green herb" for animal food (Genesis 1:30) had been changed at the Flood, at least for some animals. Similarly man was, for the first time after the Flood, permitted to eat meat (Genesis 9:3). The much harsher post-Flood environment evidently dictated such provisions, both for the sake of maintaining appropriate ecological balances in nature and also for providing the needed proteins for man and those animals that required them, since now the herbs growing from the redeposited and minerally-impoverished soils would no longer be able to provide them in adequate abundance and variety.

The psalmist at this point (verse 24) interjects a doxology in gratitude for God's power and wisdom in designing and making such wonderful provisions for the post-Flood world even through the cataclysmic destruction of another system of wonderful provisions for the pre-Flood world.

The next two verses shift from the animals on land and in the air to those in that "great and wide sea." This graphic phrase emphasizes the much more extensive oceans that were formed after the Flood by the retreating waters. All the waters once above the firmament and in the great deep below the crust were now in "*this* great and wide sea." As the land is full of God's riches (literally "acquisitions" — verse 24), so the sea also houses innumerable other living creatures. The "creeping things" are especially mentioned, no doubt the marine invertebrates of all kinds and sizes which live deep under the surface.

On the surface of the ocean, along with the ships of man's commerce, occasionally appear great monsters of the deep, to whom the wide ocean is a playground. The mysterious *leviathan* is mentioned here (also in Psalm 74:14; Job 3:8; 41:1; Isaiah 27:1). This was evidently some great marine reptile (not a crocodile, as some commentators say, since the descriptions of this animal in no way fit any crocodile or whale or any such ordinary modern animal). He is also described in these passages as a fire-breathing dragon and as a great sea serpent. It seems likely that such animals are now extinct, but the great marine sedimentary beds deposited by the Flood have yielded fossils of marine dinosaurs which would well fit the description.

Verses 27 and 28 summarize the marvelous plans and provisions God has made for every single animal He created. Although "they gather" their food, it is really God who gives it to them. When their Maker opens His hand, they are "filled with good." And, as the Lord Jesus said to His followers, "ye are of more value than many sparrows" (Luke 12:7) in the care of a loving heavenly Father.

THE PROBELM OF SUFFERING AND DEATH (Verses 29, 30)

It is true, both in the animal kingdom and in human life, that although God has made provision for life, the world is still under the bondage of struggle and death. The effects of man's sin and God's curse (Genesis 3:17-19) still shackle the whole creation. The Flood itself had constituted the greatest visitation of death on both human and animal realms the world has ever seen.

Verses 29 and 30 refer to this aspect of nature and, probably, in a specific sense to the Flood and its effects. When God, as it were, "hides His face" from His creatures, the divine power which sustains the life of the world (Acts 17:27, 28) is cut off, and they are "troubled." Then their "breath" (or "spirit") departs and their bodies disintegrate to the elements from which they had been formed.

But, though individuals — both animals and men — die,

yet life continues! Verse 30 is a remarkable testimony that God actually *creates* each new "spirit" by His own Spirit. This is primarily a reference to the "breath of life" which has been shared by both animals and men, ever since the special creation of the entity of the *nephesh,* the "living creature" or "living soul" on the fifth day of creation (Genesis 1:21). In one sense, this breath or spirit is applied individually at each birth by that same Creator. The exact nature of the "breath of life" is still completely inexplicable to the biologist, no matter how much he knows about the breathing apparatus and the blood circulation system which utilize and maintain it.

This passage, therefore, does not refer to an actual new special creation of the animals after the Flood, as some have interpreted it. The Genesis record is plain in teaching that all present land animals are descendants of those that survived the Flood in the Ark (Genesis 7:21, 22; 8:17, 19; 9:9, 10, 16).

PRAISE TO GOD FOR HIS GOODNESS
(Verses 31-35)

Our response to these wonderful provisions of God should obviously, be like that of the psalmist in the last verses of this psalm, a grateful testimony that "the glory of the Lord shall endure forever." Despite the global rebellion of wicked men and angels that caused God to send the Flood, He was not about to be, nor will He ever be, dethroned!

During the Flood, it is significant that God wished to preserve each animal "kind," as well as mankind. Though we may not yet understand exactly why He created so many different creatures, yet He did so, if for no other reason, than that it gave Him joy to do so. "The Lord shall rejoice in all His works" (verse 31). If there was joy in His creating and preserving life, however, how much greater will be His joy in seeing the love of redeemed sinners, a joy that led Him even to endure the cross (Hebrews 12:2).

The writer of the psalm (presumably David) in his glorious vision, now seeing before his enraptured eyes the awesome landscapes of the post-Flood world, noted one other feature accompanying the rising mountains and reviving plant and animal kingdoms. Though the earth would never suffer such a worldwide hydraulic upheaval again, there was still much evidence in the earth of awesome power able to unleash local convulsions in testimony of God's continuing power to judge the world. The earth was still quaking and many hills still smoking (verse 32).

There was much "residual catastrophism" for many centuries after the Flood (earth movements, volcanic activity, local floods, encroaching ice sheets, etc.) and, in fact, such activities have never altogether ceased. God's goodness is wonderfully evident everywhere in nature, but so are His power and judgment. Also, though God has promised no more worldwide hydraulic cataclysms, the continuing tectonic and volcanic activity should serve to remind man of the coming judgment by a global Fire (II Peter 3:10).

As the psalmist concludes his narrative, he is constrained by what He has seen in the creative and catastrophic works of God to give his own personal testimony in response. "I will sing unto the Lord as long as I live. I will sing praise to my God while I have my being. My meditation of Him shall be sweet. I will be glad in the Lord!"

Great numbers of men and women today are likewise finding within themselves a great heart of thanksgiving and joy in the Lord as they have come to recognize in a new way the reality of God's creation and sovereign control over this world, which has seemed to ignore Him for so long.

As the sinners once were purged from the earth by the great waters which stood over the mountains, so once again will "the sinners be consumed out of the earth" and then will "the wicked be no more." God's perfect creation will be renewed forever and therein will all His glorious purposes be fulfilled.

But then, in one final Amen, he added a great plea to all who might read it: "Praise ye the Lord!" Here is the first time this phrase (equivalent to one combined word in the Hebrew — *hallelujah*) occurs in the book of Psalms. It also is the concluding word for Psalm 105, as well as the first and last word of Psalm 106, which is the final psalm in Book IV of the book of Psalms. It then occurs as the initial and final admonition for each of the last five psalms in the entire book of Psalms. Occurring 22 times altogether in Psalms, it could be considered as a theme phrase for the book, or at least the last third of the book.

It occurs *first*, however, here at the end of this wonderful 104th Psalm. This is a natural and appropriate conclusion to any study of the glorious works of God. Hallelujah!

Chapter 10

FEARFULLY AND WONDERFULLY MADE (Psalm 139)

This familiar psalm was written by King David, after many years of fellowship with the God who had made and called him and then guided and protected him through all kinds of circumstances and in every kind of experience. The psalm has 24 verses and these divide evenly into four stanzas of six verses each. The first six verses deal with God's omniscience; the second stanza emphasizes God's omnipresence; the theme of verses 13 through 18 is that of God's omnipotence; and the last stanza stresses what might be called God's omnipurity. These four themes might be expressed this way: (1) "God knows everything about me;" (2) "God sees everything around me;" (3) "God does everything for me;" (4) "God judges everything in me."

The psalm is intensely personal, written as a prayer of David to his Lord. He uses the first person pronouns ("I," "me," "my," etc.) no less than 48 times in these 24 verses. In speaking to God, he uses the second person ("thou," "thee," "thine," etc.) 28 times, and, in addition, he cries "O Lord," three times and "O God" three times.

David's experiences, of course, parallel in many respects those of every other believer, so that we could all well appropriate both his testimonies and his prayers as our own. No doubt, in fact, this is exactly what the Holy

Spirit intended us to do, at least with many of the psalms, and this is why He included them in the Holy Scriptures which he inspired. Psalm 139 is an especially thrilling example of a psalm of great blessing and encouragement, as well as exhortation, to the Christian today.

THE OMNISCIENCE OF GOD
(Verses 1-6)

David exhausts every superlative in describing how God knows absolutely everything there is to know about him — more, even, than he knew about himself. And if God knew one person so intimately, He would also know everything about every other person as well. Since human beings are the most complex systems in the universe, it follows that God knows everything about all less complex systems, too. In short, He is omniscient!

"O Lord thou hast searched me and known me. Thou knowest my downsitting and mine uprising, thou understandest my thought afar off." Not only does the Lord know everything we do, He also understands everything we think. Nor is He like some human mentalist, who supposedly can read the minds of people near him. God knows our thoughts no matter where we are, and even before they enter our own minds! That is why He can say: ". . . your Father knoweth what things ye have need of, before ye ask Him" (Matthew 6:8).

"Thou compasseth my path, and my lying down, and art acquainted with all my ways." Whether rising or walking or sitting or lying down, the Lord is fully aware, moment by moment, of everything in which we are involved. The path we follow is all explored for us ahead of time because God has, as it were, "sifted" (a more precise meaning than "compassed") it out with His divine sieve, removing any insuperable obstacles or unavoidable pitfalls, before we travel it.

"For there is not a word in my tongue, but, lo, O Lord, thou knowest it all together." If God anticipates even

our very thoughts, it is no very great thing if He hears all our words. But words affect other people, and therefore Jesus said: "But I say unto you, that every idle word that men shall speak they shall give account thereof in the day of judgment. For by thy words thou shalt be justified, and by thy words thou shalt be condemned" (Matthew 12:36, 37).

"Thou hast set me behind and before, and laid thine hand upon me." God knows what lies ahead of us, what has happened in our wake after us, and has His guiding and constraining hand upon us each present moment. Future, past, and present are alike in His understanding since He is the Creator even of Time itself — therefore, controlling all that can ever happen during time.

David concludes this stanza by confessing: *"Such knowledge is too wonderful for me: It is high, I cannot attain unto it."* How many people have engaged in endless and pointless controversy over the wonders of God's foreknowledge and election in relation to man's freedom and responsibility! We should remember that "as the heavens are higher than the earth, so are my ways higher than your ways, and my thoughts than your thoughts" (Isaiah 55:9). We can rejoice in the assurance of God's foreordaining efforts on our behalf, as the psalmist does here, but we cannot comprehend them. Such knowledge is too wonderful for our minds, and we cannot attain unto it.

GOD'S OMNIPRESENCE (Verses 7-12)

It does seem a little easier for us to grasp the concept of space than of time, and we are thus a little more comfortable with the fact that God is everywhere in space than we are in contemplating the divine contemporaneity of all events in time. In any case, David proceeds in the next stanza of the psalm to discuss the impossibility of going anywhere to escape the presence of God.

"Whither shall I go from thy spirit? or whither shall I

flee from thy presence?" These parallel questions are obviously rhetorical. The Holy Spirit is omnipresent. "Do not I fill heaven and earth? saith the Lord" (Jeremiah 23:24). Even if it were humanly possible to build a spaceship to carry us out to the very end of space, or a tunneling projectile to convey us to the center of the earth, God would be awaiting us there. As David expressed it: *"If I ascend up into heaven, thou art there: If I make my bed in hell, behold thou art there."*

"If I take the wings of the morning, and dwell in the uttermost parts of the sea." The "wings of the morning" refers to the east, the "uttermost parts of the [Mediterranean] sea" to the west. Whether up to heaven or down to hell, whether infinitely east or infinitely west — wherever one could conceive of ever going or being — *"Even there shall thy hand lead me, and thy right hand shall hold me."*

One can never be hidden from God's all-seeing eye. *"If I say, Surely the darkness shall cover me; even the night shall be light about me."* After all, God is light, and "the light shineth in darkness" (John 1:5). Darkness and light cannot coexist in the same space and God is omnipresent and "in Him is no darkness at all" (I John 1:5). *"Yea, the darkness hideth not from thee; but the night shineth as the day: the darkness and the light are both alike to thee."* "He revealeth the deep and secret things: He knoweth what is in the darkness, and the light dwelleth with Him" (Daniel 2:22). Indeed, "all things are naked and opened unto the eyes of Him with whom we have to do" (Hebrews 4:13).

THE CREATION OF THE HUMAN BODY
(Verses 13-18)

Verses 13 through 18 stress the omnipotence of God, focusing especially on His creation of the human body and its ability for reproduction and multiplication.

Man's body is, by far, the most complex and intricately designed system in the universe. The absurd notion that such a marvelous organism could have developed slowly over the ages by random processes of evolution is a graphic commentary on man's desire to escape from God at all costs.

To the one whose heart and mind are open to God, his own body is a continual witness to the power and wisdom of God. *"For thou hast possessed my reins* [that is, literally, 'my kidneys,' stressing both the inmost emotions and also the marvelous physiologic provision for daily renewal and cleansing of the body]: *thou hast covered me in my mother's womb."* The word "covered" is the same as "shielded," and refers to the amazingly efficient design of a protective chamber in which the fragile embryonic body can develop, cushioned hydraulically from injury, yet continuously sustained and fed through the mother's body.

"I will praise thee: for I am fearfully and wonderfully made: marvelous are thy works: and that my soul knoweth right well." The "works" of God are a testimony to His power. In fact, modern science equates the accomplishment of the work required to produce any system or to maintain any process with the expenditure of energy and, therefore, with the continual availability of power, and this must ultimately be the omnipotence of God Himself. But mere power is not sufficient — there must also be "information," to direct the application of the power in producing complex systems. Higher organisms, especially man, could never be produced by the simple availability of raw energy from the sun or any other source. It must be *directed* energy, guided by an information program containing all the specifications on how to proceed.

And this is exactly what the psalmist is speaking of. When he considers the production of his own body, he marvels that he is so "wonderfully" made. The word actually is "differently," stressing the amazing fact that each individual is quite unique and distinct from all others, in spite of his development by a process common to all.

Next comes a marvelous verse, long anticipating modern science. *"My substance was not hid from thee, when I was made in secret, and curiously wrought in the lowest parts of the earth."* There is a somewhat parallel passage in Ecclesiastes 11:5: "As thou knowest not what is the way of the spirit, nor how the bones do grow in the womb of her that is with child: even so thou knowest not the works of God who maketh all."

The word "substance" could well be rendered "frame," and refers to the complete structure of the adult person. The full-grown body had actually been planned, designed, and programmed when it was not even large enough to be visible, in the "unseen parts of the earth." The mysterious process was one of "embroidering" (the literal meaning of the striking phrase "curiously wrought" is "embroidered"). It is as though a form were being sewed onto an intricate and beautiful pattern already laid out. This is an accurate description of the remarkable process of embryonic growth as delineated by modern molecular biology. The pattern in the DNA molecule is an intricate double-helical structure, which serves as a template for specifying and building up, cell by cell, the final adult body. It is an amazing process, which modern geneticists are only beginning to understand, but it was outlined here in Scripture almost three thousand years before it began to be understood at all.

"Thine eyes did see my substance yet being unperfect." The latter phrase ("substance yet being unperfect") is actually one word, meaning "embryo." *"In thy book all my members were written, which in continuance were fashioned when as yet there was none of them."* The word "continuance" is the Hebrew word "days" and the word "fashioned" is "formed" — the same word used in the account of man's creation, when God "formed" man of the dust of the earth. The phrase "my members" is not in the original. Thus, the meaning

of this verse is somewhat as follows: "All the events of my days had been formed and written down in thy book before I was ever conceived."

That is, not only has God designed all things in space, He had planned all events in time. We indeed are fearfully and wonderfully made! No wonder the psalmist exclaims: *"How precious also are thy thoughts unto me, O God! how great is the sum of them!"* By God's omniscience were all things planned and by His omnipotence were all His plans implemented, under the all-seeing eye of His omnipresence.

And since God knows our thoughts (verse 2), we should desire to know His thoughts. They are "precious" and "great in sum." It is significant that this was the purpose of the truly great scientists such as Isaac Newton — that is, to "think God's thoughts after Him." So likewise it should be our desire to "bring into captivity every thought to the obedience of Christ" (II Corinthians 10:5). There is no danger that such concentration of our thoughts on His thoughts (and these, of course, are available to us both in His Word and in His world) would ever be limited or circumscribed. *"If I should count them, they are more in number than the sand: when I awake, I am still with thee."*

THE HOLINESS OF GOD
(Verses 19-24)

Now some might conclude that, since God has planned everything long before it happened, those deeds which are evil were also planned and thus will be excused by God. But not only is God perfect in knowledge and power and present everywhere in space and time, He is also perfect in holiness. He can, therefore, by no means condone wickedness forever. *"Surely thou wilt slay the wicked, O God: depart from me therefore, ye bloody men* [or 'men of blood']." These final six verses of Psalm 139 emphasize God's omnipurity and His demand for His people to separate from all ungodliness and from all ungodly associations.

"For they speak against thee wickedly, and thine enemies take thy name in vain." The very essence of wickedness is to speak against God and His Word, or to treat them with lightness; this attitude is the precursor of all other sins. It is presumptuous to question any of the attributes of God's sovereignty such as those emphasized in this very psalm. But it is even greater presumption to use God's sovereignty, as some do, to excuse sin. Even though in our finite minds we cannot understand how to reconcile God's sovereignty with man's responsibility (as verse 6 indicates, "such knowledge is too wonderful for me"), they are both absolutely real and true. We can rejoice, as David did, in the glories of His never-failing guidance and presence and power, and yet tremble at the reality of His judgment.

"Do not I hate them, O Lord, that hate thee? and am not I grieved with those that rise up against thee?" The latter expression is, literally, "I loathe them!" The believer must not only put away sin in his own life, but must discern and hate sin as God does.

But how is this attitude to be reconciled with Christ's command to "love your enemies" (Matthew 5:44)? The next verse even says: *"I hate them with perfect hatred: I count them mine enemies."*

There can be no contradiction in God's Word, of course. We are to love *our* enemies, but hate *His* enemies! And we are to hate them with *perfect* hatred — that is, we must hate sin as God does and seek to think His thoughts on *this* matter also. But just as there is a glorious paradox in the relation between God's sovereignty and man's freedom, so there is a similar grand paradox between God's perfect hatred of wicked men and His perfect love of redeemed men. Believers likewise are to exhibit both perfect hatred and "perfect love, which casteth out fear" (I John 4:18). Furthermore, even a perfect hatred of those who "hate thee" (verse 21) can never contradict God's sacrificial love for lost men. "But

God commendeth His love toward us, in that, while we were yet sinners, Christ died for us" (Romans 5:8).

The psalm closes with one of the greatest prayers of the Bible. The natural response of one who has caught a glimpse of God's glory and majesty, as David had done in this psalm, is to become acutely aware of his own sinfulness and to seek forgiveness and cleansing. When righteous Job saw the Lord, he cried out: "I abhor myself, and repent in dust and ashes" (Job 42:6).

The same with David. Having meditated on God's omniscience, experienced His onmipresence, marveled at His omnipotence, and realized His perfect holiness, he could only pray: "*Search me, O God, and know my heart; try me, and know my thoughts.*"

But the prayer had already been answered! In verse 1 he had testified "thou hast searched me" and in verse 2, he had acknowledged "thou understandest my thought afar off."

"*And see if there be any wicked way in me, and lead me in the way everlasting.*" In verse 3, David had also recognized that "thou art acquainted with all my ways." The intent of the prayer obviously was not merely to urge God to search his mind and heart and to examine his ways, because he well knew that God had already done all this. Like all the rest of his psalm, this really is an expression of his desire to know the mind of God Himself — to know even his *own* heart as God knows it.

And when we can finally understand as God understands, thinking His thoughts after Him, not only about His great creation, but even about our own sinfulness and need of His salvation, then He truly is leading us in the way everlasting.

Chapter 11

SCIENTIFIC GLEANINGS IN OTHER PSALMS

In this section, we have examined in some detail eight of the greatest psalms and their scientific revelations and implications. There are far too many psalms to allow a similar verse-by-verse treatment of all them within the scope of this book, but we can at least look at a few other scattered verses with scientific significance.

For example, the tremendous extent of the universe is implied in Psalm 103:11, 12:

> For as the heaven is high above the earth, so great is His mercy toward them that fear Him. As far as the east is from the west, so far hath He removed our transgressions from us.

These wonderful verses assure us of God's full forgiveness of the sins of His people, and it is significant that He compares this to the infinite height of the heavens. In other words, rather than viewing the starry heavens as a solid vaulted dome at some fixed distance above the earth, as many ancient peoples did, the psalmist realized the depths of space were so vast they could not be even imagined, and so provided an adequate simile for the greatness of God's mercy.

Similarly, instead of considering the eastern edge of the flat earth to be at some finite distance from its western edge, he understood that one could travel eastward or westward forever. This means either that he viewed the extent of space as infinite or, more likely, the earth as round!

The universal principle of decay is also mentioned in this psalm:

> For He knoweth our frame; He remembereth that we are dust. As for man, his days are as grass: as a flower of the field, so he flourisheth. For the wind passeth over it, and it is gone; and the place thereof shall know it no more (Psalm 103:14-16).

The universal experience of death and disintegration is, of course, a matter of common observation, but it may not be so obvious that the deaths of men and animals are part of a common law obeyed by grass and flowers as well.

Still more remarkable is the fact that this zoological and botanical phenomenon is shared with the heavens and the earth. All obey a common law, now known as the Second Law of Thermodynamics, one of the most fundamental and universal principles of modern science. This significant fact is recognized in the previous psalm:

> Of old hast thou laid the foundation of the earth: and the heavens are the work of thy hands. They shall perish, but thou shalt endure: yea, all of them shall wax old like a garment; as a vesture shalt thou change them, and they shall be changed (Psalm 102:25, 26).

That every process — whether cosmic or terrestrial, organic or inorganic — is in bondage to this principle of decay and death is one of the greatest discoveries of modern science. It was also foreshadowed in these and other Bible passages three thousand years ago!

Another important scientific truth — not yet admitted by many scientists, but nevertheless confirmed by all hard scientific observations now available — is that this planet Earth is uniquely the abode of human life. No other planet in the solar system is capable of supporting life, as the space program has conclusively shown, and no other star has been yet observed with planets of any kind.

This exclusive domain of mankind is intimated in Psalm 115:16:

The heaven, even the heavens, are the Lord's: but the earth hath He given to the children of men.

The same limitation is suggested in Psalm 8:3, 4, as well as Genesis 1:26-29, Acts 17:24-27, John 3:13, and other passages.

Related to the question of extraterrestrial life is the question of the origin of life. Evolutionists would love to find evidence of the evolution of life in other parts of the universe to help justify their belief in its naturalistic origin here on earth. But life is far too complex to have evolved from nonliving chemicals even one time, let alone many times! This was pointed out in Psalm 139, discussed in the preceding chapter. Only God, who *is* life, can create life! This is confirmed in Psalm 36:9:

For with thee is the fountain of life: in thy light shall we see light.

Similarly, modern evolutionists believe that the naturalistic evolutionary process has developed the heavens and the earth, as well as plants and animals and man. Many evolutionists even maintain that evolution has "come to consciousness," as it were, in man, who now himself can program further evolutionary progress for future men. The absurdity of such conceit is emphasized frequently in the psalms.

For example, Psalms 95-100 comprise a unitary group of psalms of praise and triumph. Repeatedly these emphasize the fact that the Lord Himself made the various components of creation.

The sea is His, and He made it: and His hands formed the dry land (Psalm 95:5).

For all the gods of the nations are idols: but the Lord made the heavens (Psalm 96:5).

Know ye that the Lord he is God: it is He that hath made us, and not we ourselves: we are His people, and the sheep of His pasture (Psalm 100:3).

Similarly, Psalm 136 stresses that God *alone* is responsible for the making of all things; exhorting men to give thanks to Him.

> To Him who alone doeth great wonders: . . . .
> To Him that by wisdom made the heavens: . . . .
> To Him that stretched out the earth above the waters: . . . . To Him that made great lights: . . . . The sun to rule by day: . . . . The moon and stars to rule by night: . . . (Psalm 136: 4-9).

There is certainly no Biblical warrant for the strange doctrine of "theistic" evolution. Furthermore, there is not one iota of scientific evidence for evolution, either.

> For I know that the Lord is great, and that our Lord is above all gods. Whatsoever the Lord pleased, that did He in heaven, and in earth, in the seas, and all deep places. He causeth the vapours to ascend from the ends of the earth; He maketh lightnings for the rain; He bringeth the wind out of His treasuries (Psalm 135:5-7).

The last two verses even anticipate the interrelationships of the phenomena of evaporation, atmospheric electricity, rain, and the global atmospheric circulation with the deep lakes and oceans in earth's marvelous postdiluvian weather structure.

A number of other scientific inferences will be discussed in some of the psalms to be examined in later sections (e.g., Psalms 40, 147, 148). There are numerous other references in the Psalms to the creation, to natural phenomena, to human nature, and to other things which are of direct interest to modern scientists. It is bound to be significant, especially in view of the many anticipatory scientific insights already discussed, that not one of these when properly interpreted contains any scientific mistake. No wonder the psalmist could say, as can the humble believer today:

> I have more understanding than all my teachers: for thy testimonies are my meditation (Psalm 119:99).

PART THREE

THE PSALMS AND
THE SAVIOR

Chapter 12
THE SON OF GOD
(Psalm 2)

In one sense, practically all the psalms could be understood as prophetic of the coming Savior. In type, if nothing else, each one seems to foreshadow in one way or another either "the sufferings of Christ" or "the glory that should follow" (I Peter 1:11).

There are a number of psalms, however, which are so explicitly clear in their description of the person or works of Christ that practically all Bible-believing Christian writers after Christ, as well as even some Jewish rabbis before Christ, have recognized them as peculiarly "Messianic" psalms. Their prophetic descriptions are so accurate as to be outside the range of speculative probabilities, and thus they provide uniquely powerful evidence of divine inspiration.

The first, and one of the greatest, of these Messianic psalms is Psalm 2, the psalm immediately following the great introductory psalm. The two groups of mankind categorized in Psalm 1 quickly become personalized in Psalm 2 in a great council of Christ-hating leaders arrayed against Christ and His followers.

The second Psalm is unique among the psalms in three interesting respects. It is actually referred to by number in the New Testament (Acts 13:33), a fact which indicates that the chapter divisions were present in the Book of Psalms right from the start. Secondly, its Davidic authorship is confirmed in the New Testament (Acts

4:25), even though the heading of the psalm itself, contrary to the usual situation, does not say who the author is.

This psalm is also one of the greatest of the Messianic psalms. It is one of the very few Old Testament passages — and the only one in the psalms — which refers by name to the Son of God (verses 7, 12). The psalm is written in the form of a great dramatic poem, in four stanzas of three verses each. The first stanza is written directly in terms of David's perspective; the second stanza stresses the viewpoint of God the Father; the third is in the form of a direct statement by God the Son; the final stanza is a testimony which most appropriately would come from God the Holy Spirit.

THE KINGS OF THE EARTH
(Verses 1-3)

In the first stanza, it is as though David were carried forward in the Spirit to a future time. In his vision, he sees great assemblages of people coming together, perhaps in many different times and places, and, as he listens to their speeches and deliberations, he is greatly disturbed and perplexed at what he hears. Finally, he cries out: "Why?"

"*Why do the heathen rage, and the people imagine a vain thing?*" The word "heathen" refers especially to the Gentile nations, and "people" (by parallelism) to the people of those nations and probably of the Jewish nation as well. The word "rage" is, literally, "tumultuously assemble." Evidently the people of various nations are coming together, through their representatives, in a great convocation, and they are boisterous and riotous. Their purpose is to "imagine" (literally, "study" or "plan") a "vain thing." The latter phrase is one word in the Hebrew, but the translation is accurate.

And what is the vain thing which the nations are planning? "*The kings of the earth set themselves, and the rulers take counsel together against the Lord, and*

against His anointed." The word "anointed," of course,
is *Messiah*, the Hebrew equivalent of the Greek *Christ*.
Thus the assembly has been called together to plan a
concerted rebellion and opposition against Jehovah and
against Jesus Christ!

The prophecy was fulfilled in a precursive way at the
trial of Christ. After quoting this very verse, the early
church then applied it thus: "For of a truth against thy
holy child Jesus, whom thou hast anointed, both Herod
and Pontius Pilate, with the Gentiles, and the people of
Israel, were gathered together" (Acts 4:27).

The ultimate fulfillment, however, will no doubt be at
the very end of the age, in the last great rebellion against
God, of both men and devils. "For they are the spirits of
devils, working miracles, which go forth unto the kings
of the earth and of the whole world, to gather them to the
battle of that great day of God Almighty" (Revelation
16:14). This "gathering together" is to Armageddon
(Revelation 16:16), but there is even another such
assemblage after the millennium. "[Satan] shall go out
to deceive the nations which are in the four quarters of
the earth, Gog and Magog, to gather them together to
battle . . ." (Revelation 20:8).

Between the initial fulfillment of this prophecy, at the
trial of Christ, and the final fulfillment at the end of the
age, there have been innumerable other partial fulfill-
ments. The word "rulers" in verse 2 can be applied to
leaders of any sort. Whenever there is an educational
convocation, a scientific convention, a political confer-
ence, an industrial gathering, the almost universal practice is to ignore the leadership of God and His Christ
and, in some cases, actively to oppose them. Men
operate under the awful delusion that they can plan and
decide things on their own, without consulting the will of
God.

Perhaps the most conspicuous example is the Assembly of the United Nations. Another was the great Dar-
winian Centennial Convocation in 1959 at the University
of Chicago, where the convocation keynote speaker, Sir

Julian Huxley, boasted that "Darwinism had removed the very concept of God from the sphere of rational discussion." More recently, the American Humanist Association, in its 1974 Manifesto, blatantly declared: "No deity will save us, we will save ourselves."

The essential man-centered theme of all such assemblies is, as David foresaw, *"Let us break their bands asunder, and cast away their cords from us."* What little restraint is still practiced among men because of the fear of God must be fully removed. God and His Word, Christ and His salvation, must be banished from the schools, from the airwaves, from the press, and an atheistic bondage (such as now exists in most of the world's nations) replace the bonds of love and cords of compassion which constrain all who serve God.

Truly, this is a *vain thing* which the people *imagine*! "Because that, when they knew God, they glorified Him not as God, neither were thankful; but became *vain in their imaginations*, and their foolish heart was darkened. Professing themselves to be wise, they became fools" (Romans 1:21, 22).

HEAVENLY DERISION (Verses 4-6)

One of the most tragic verses in all the Bible opens the second stanza of this psalm. *"He that sitteth in the heavens shall laugh: the Lord shall have them in derision."* When men take counsel to dethrone God, it hardly provokes Him to fear or flight! It provokes Him to derisive laughter. The fact that men foolishly reject God as their Creator does not mean He did not really create them. "Because I have called, and ye refused; I have stretched out my hand, and no man regarded; But ye have set at naught all my counsel, and would none of my reproof; I also will laugh at your calamity; I will mock when your fear cometh" (Proverbs 1:24-26).

The scene thus shifts in this stanza to the heavens, where God the Father sits on the throne. After laughing at the fools who say there is no God (Psalm 14:1), *then*

He speaks. "*Then shall He speak unto them in His wrath, and vex them in His sore displeasure.*" First, He laughs at them, then speaks to them, and finally "troubles" them. There is coming a day of "vengeance on them that know not God, and that obey not the gospel of our Lord Jesus Christ" (II Thessalonians 1:8).

When God finally does break His long and patient silence, these will be His words: "*Yet have I set my king upon my holy hill of Zion.*" Though men would take counsel together and plot against the Lord, finally even condemning His anointed one to be crucified, it was all merely in the accomplishment of God's plan, "For to do whatever thy hand and thy counsel determined before to be done" (Acts 4:28).

There are two senses, of course, in which God will set His king upon the hill of Zion. The word used for "set" actually means either "offer" or "pour out." It is translated "offer," for example, in Psalm 16:4. "Their drink offerings of blood will I not offer." Thus, the reference here is first of all to God's offering of His anointed one on Mount Zion, pouring out His blood in atonement for sin. What divine irony! When men and devils took counsel together to put the Savior to death, it was only that "through death He might destroy him that had the power of death, that is, the devil" (Hebrews 2:14).

But then also He will be anointed on Mount Zion not only for death, but as King. "Rejoice greatly, O daughter of Zion; . . . behold, thy King cometh unto thee" (Zechariah 9:9). "And it shall be in that day, that living waters shall go out from Jerusalem; . . . . And the Lord shall be king over all the earth" (Zechariah 14:8, 9). "For out of Zion shall go forth the law, and the word of the Lord from Jerusalem" (Isaiah 2:3).

THE SON OF GOD SPEAKS
(Verses 7-9)

In the third stanza is heard the voice of the Son of God, the one who had been offered up as a sacrifice on the holy hill of Zion, the one against whom the world's leaders would take counsel together, whose cords they would, age after age, seek to unloose. If there was a mystery concerning how He could be anointed both as sacrifice and king, it is resolved in this stanza. He would not only suffer death, but would, in the process, *conquer death!*

"*I will declare the decree.*" "No man hath seen God at any time; the only begotten Son, which is in the bosom of the Father, he hath declared Him" (John 1: 18). The Father made the decree, the Son declared it. He is the *Word* of God, and when we hear Him, we hear the Father. And what is that decree?

He quotes from the Father: "*The Lord hath said unto me, Thou art my Son; this day have I begotten thee.*" There are several senses in which Jesus Christ is the only-begotten Son of God, but here the emphasis is on His resurrection from the dead. He had been condemned and crucified, and, if that had been all, no one would have believed on Him. But He was "declared to be the Son of God with power . . . by the resurrection from the dead" (Romans 1:4). He was the "firstborn from the dead" (Colossians 1:18). He is "the faithful witness, and the first begotten of the dead, and the prince of the kings of the earth" (Revelation 1:18).

Any question that this verse refers to His resurrection is dispelled by its quotation in the New Testament: "And we declare unto you glad tidings, how that the promise which was made unto the fathers, God hath fulfilled the same unto us their children, in that He hath raised up Jesus again, as it is also written in the second psalm, Thou art my Son, this day have I begotten thee" (Acts 13:32-33). This same verse is also quoted in Hebrews 5:5.

Because of His victory over death, He will triumph over all lesser enemies. Continuing His declaration of God's decree, He quotes the Father: "*Ask of me, and I shall give thee the heathen* [or 'nations'] *for thine inheritance, and the uttermost parts of the earth for thy possession.*" The Son is also the Heir, and He is to be "heir of all things" (Hebrews 1:2). Since He "created all things" (Colossians 1:16), is "upholding all things" (Hebrews 1:3), and died to "reconcile all things" (Colossians 1:20), therefore, eventually He will "gather together in one all things in Christ" (Ephesians 1:10).

"Thou shalt break them with a rod of iron, thou shalt dash them in pieces like a potter's vessel." The kings and rulers and leaders of the earth, with few exceptions, will not submit willingly unto Him, and so He must "put down all rule and all authority and power" (I Corinthians 15:24). "And out of His mouth goeth a sharp sword, that with it He should smite the nations: and He shall rule them with a rod of iron: and He treadeth the winepress of the fierceness and wrath of Almighty God" (Revelation 19:15). Furthermore, those who are His followers shall share in His reign. "And he that overcometh, and keepeth my works unto the end, to him will I give power over the nations: And he shall rule them with a rod of iron; as the vessels of a potter shall they be broken to shivers: even as I received of my Father" (Revelation 2:26, 27). These great promises will, so far as we can tell from Scripture, all be fulfilled literally in the coming Tribulation and Millennium periods. The Good Shepherd shall constrain all rebels in the flock with a rod of iron.

THE EXHORTATION (Verses 10-12)

The last trilogy of verses contains an exhortation, a warning, and an invitation. Though the psalmist does not say so specifically, it is appropriate to think of these as the direct urgings of God the Holy Spirit. It is His ministry to "reprove the world of sin, and of righteousness, and of judgment:" (John 16:8), and that is exactly what these verses do.

"Be wise now therefore, O ye kings: be instructed, ye judges of the earth." The emphasis is on *now*. Don't persist in your rebellion until that day when every knee shall be forced to bow, and every tongue compelled to

confess Christ as Lord. "Behold, now is the accepted time; behold, now is the day of salvation" (II Corinthians 6:2). The kings and ruler who vainly imagine they can do away with God and His Christ, though professing themselves to be wise, have become fools, for "fools despise wisdom and instruction" (Proverbs 1:7).

"Serve the Lord with fear, and rejoice with trembling." These are parallels and are strongly emotional terms. Serving the Lord is joyful, but is to be with great reverence and holy awe. "Wherefore we receiving a kingdom which cannot be moved, let us have grace, whereby we may serve God acceptably with reverence and godly fear" (Hebrews 12:28).

"Kiss the Son, lest He be angry, and ye perish from the way, when His wrath is kindled but a little." This is the other Hebrew word for "son." In verse 7 it is *ben*; here it is *bar*. There is no doubt, however, that both verses identify Him as the Son of God. Some versions (e.g., Revised Standard, Living Bible, etc.) either replace or modify this command by "kiss his feet," but such a translation reveals more about the bias, than the skill, of the translators. The "kiss" is one of true and selfless love. Not only are men to serve the Lord, but also to love the Lord. "If any man love not the Lord Jesus Christ, let him be Anathema Maranatha" (literally "accursed, for our Lord is coming") (I Corinthians 16:22).

The word for "but a little" is also, in other passages, rendered "soon," and it may be that such is the emphasis here. The day of the "wrath of the Lamb" (Revelation 6:16) is soon coming, and then it will be too late. Men should be wise *now*, therefore!

This great psalm concludes with a beautiful gospel invitation: *"Blessed* [or 'happy'] *are all they that put their trust in Him."* This invitation, down through the ages, has been accepted and proved by many kings and leaders, even by evolutionists and atheists, as well as by multitudes of ordinary "people" in all "nations." It is still a promise in God's Word and will still prove true today, for all who believe.

Chapter 13

THE GARDEN PRAYER AND THE EMPTY TOMB
(Psalm 16)

The greatest event in history since the very creation of the world itself, as well as the crowning proof of the truth of Christianity, is the bodily resurrection of the Lord Jesus Christ. Psalm 16 contains a thrilling prophecy of this resurrection, written by David a thousand years before its fulfillment. As the apostles went forth to preach after Christ's ascension, in accordance with His Great Commission, the record tells that "with great power gave the apostles witness of the resurrection of the Lord Jesus: and great grace was upon them all" (Acts 4:33). Furthermore, they referred to the Scriptures (Acts 13:35-37) and used this psalm as the keystone of their preaching that the Scriptures foretold Christ's resurrection. We are, therefore, well justified in applying the psalm to Christ. Indeed, it is one of the greatest of all the Messianic psalms.

One of the first things to note is that, although Psalm 16 is written by David in the first person, no doubt against a background of his own experiences, it goes far beyond anything that could be applied merely to him. It clearly is a prayer from the very heart of Christ, and we should read it as though Christ Himself is speaking the words.

THE GARDEN OF GETHSEMANE
(Verses 1-4)

Although He speaks of the resurrection (verse 10), it is evident that the resurrection is placed in the future tense. Thus, the prayer predates the resurrection and, for that matter, evidently predates the cross as well. Yet both the cross and the empty tomb are clearly in the very immediate future. All things considered, the context fits perfectly the conclusion that this psalm can be nothing less than the prayer uttered by Christ in the Garden of Gethsemane, the night before His crucifixion. The exposition below will proceed on that assumption.

He had just prayed: "O my Father, if this cup may not pass away from me except I drink it, thy will be done" (Matthew 26:42). Having accepted the bitter cup, He then turned Himself over to the care of His loving Father:

"Preserve me, O God: for in thee do I put my trust. O my soul, thou hast said unto the Lord, Thou art my Lord: my goodness extendeth not to thee" (verse 1, 2). That is, though He was holy and sinless, He was not offering His goodness to God as justification for escaping the wrath of God deserved by sinners. For He Himself was about to be "made sin for us, who knew no sin, that we might be made the righteousness of God in Him" (II Corinthians 5:21).

Instead of offering His righteousness to God, it was to be offered *"to the saints that are in the earth, and to the excellent, in whom is all my delight"* (verse 3). It was His delight to offer the free gift of His own righteousness to those whose hearts desired forgiveness, the "saints" (that is, the "ones set apart") and the "excellent" (those who would gladly respond to His grace and love, and to whom thus could be imputed His own excellence).

On the other hand, there would be many others who

would not have Him. They would, instead, *"hasten after another god"* (literally, "exchange for others"). There would be many excuses offered, and many other ways tried, to avoid responding to Him. But, since His righteousness is the only righteousness acceptable before a holy God, the end of all such dissimulating can only be that *"their sorrows will be multiplied."* Ever since the great Curse on the ground (Genesis 3:17), the lot of fallen man has been one of sorrow. Christ has offered deliverance from sorrow and death, but for those who reject Him there can only be left an endless multiplication of sorrows.

Not that such people were irreligious. Sacrifices and offerings without end have always been found among those who reject Christ — even *"drink offerings of blood,"* as though the gods were thirsty for the blood of men and beasts! These were utterly repugnant, however, to the Savior.

Yet He, Himself, was about to drink the bitterest cup of all, and to offer up His own precious blood, in order that God's holiness might be vindicated, and yet sinners be saved. There were, indeed, drink offerings prescribed in the Mosaic Laws (Numbers 15:7), and even before the time of Moses (Genesis 35:14), but these were of wine, not blood, the wine symbolizing the blood which he would one day shed on the cross. Furthermore, these drink offerings were to be "poured out" at the altar, not drunk, as the heathen did them. The people of Israel were specifically forbidden to eat or drink blood — the blood was given on the altar as an atonement for their souls (Leviticus 17:11- 14), not as some mystical source of life and power, as the heathen believed.

For such as these, He could not *"take up their names into my lips."* For each one who would truly confess His name, however, He would turn gladly to "confess his name before my Father" (Revelation 3:5).

THE CUP AND THE HERITAGE
(Verses 5-8)

The next three verses (5-7) seem particularly appropriate in the context of Christ's prayer to His Father concerning the "cup" which He was to drink and the comfort and assurance granted to Him, even in light of that dread prospect. Verse 5 even mentions the cup: *"The Lord is the portion of my inheritance and of my cup: thou maintainest my lot."*

When the tribes of Israel entered the promised land, each family received a certain "lot," determined by the "casting of lots," to serve as its inheritance. Jesus Christ, however, in His humanity never had a home, or even any place to "lay His head" (Matthew 8:20). The Lord was *His* inheritance, and that was sufficient. Furthermore, that lot was kept up and assured also by the Lord. ". . . the Father hath not left me alone; for I do always those things that please Him: (John 8:29).

But that inheritance involved a "cup" as well, — a word which comprehended one's entire life experience, especially that portion of his experience which might involve testing or suffering. The specific cup which was to be taken by the Lord Jesus was the most bitter cup ever offered, that containing the wine of God's wrath against the sin of the world (Revelation 14:19; Matthew 26:27, 28).

And yet He, "for the joy that was set before Him, endured the cross, despising the shame" (Hebrews 12:2). In spite of all the infinite suffering He must endure in order to redeem lost men, He could look forward to the great inheritance awaiting Him beyond the cross.

"The lines [that is, the surveying lines outlining the "lot" of His inheritance] *are fallen unto me in pleasant places; yea, I have a goodly heritage"* (verse 6).

His inheritance is nothing less than the entire world of the redeemed. "I shall give thee the nations for thine inheritance, and the uttermost parts of the earth for thy possession" (Psalm 2:8). Indeed, He is to be "appointed heir of all things" (Hebrews 1:2). And because He drank the cup on our behalf, we have the inestimable privilege of being "heirs of God, and joint heirs with Christ" (Romans 8:17).

In the Gospel accounts, it is recorded that, after His ordeal of prayer and travail that night in the Garden of Gethsemane, when even "His sweat was as it were great drops of blood falling down to the ground" (Luke 22:44), "there appeared an angel unto Him from heaven, strengthening Him" (Luke 22:43). It is apparently this event that is prophesied in verse 7 of the psalm. *"I will bless the Lord, who hath given me counsel: my reins also instruct me in the night seasons."*

THE BODILY RESURRECTION
(Verses 8-11)

The last four verses of the psalm (all quoted in Acts 2:25-28) do contain a remarkable summary of the events following the prayer in the Garden, especially His death and resurrection. Immediately after the prayer, Judas came and He was arrested and taken to prison and judgment. The several pseudo-trials that followed, accompanied by insults and mockery and, finally, beatings and condemnation to death, were unjust in the extreme, yet He bore it patiently and without resistance. This is all implied in verse 8 *"I have set the Lord always before me: because He is at my right hand, I shall not be moved."* He had no public defender or counsel — only accusers and judges. Nevertheless, the Lord was both before Him for protection and at His right hand for guidance, so that He was not alone.

As a result of His Father's assurance and presence, He could look forward with joy even to the experience of death itself. *"Therefore my heart is glad and my glory rejoiceth."* The word "glory," following the Septuagint, is rendered by the word "tongue" in Peter's quotation of this verse in Acts 2:26 — "my tongue is glad."

This might seem like an unusual interchange of meanings, especially if ordinary men were in view. For such

men, their tongues are hardly instruments of glory! In
fact, James says: "But the tongue can no man tame; it is
an unruly evil, full of deadly poison" (James 3:8). Of the
Lord Jesus, however, even His enemies testified: "Never
man spake like this man" (John 7:46). Another
psalmist, speaking prophetically of this same man, said:
"Thou art fairer than the children of men: grace is
poured into thy lips" (Psalm 45:2). Of the one who was
the very Word of God incarnate, speaking words which
would last forever (Matthew 24:35), it is beautifully
fitting to equate His tongue with His glory!

"My flesh also shall rest in hope." After His trial and
His death would come His burial, with the battered flesh
of His body resting in Joseph's tomb. However, that
body would not return to dust, even though every other
dead body since the beginning of time had so disinte-
grated. *His* body would merely rest until His spirit returned to it after accomplishing a vital mission in the
heart of the earth. His ministry of substitution and
propitiation would have already been fully accomplished on the cross, as testified by the victory cry, "It is
finished!" (John 19:30) immediately before He withdrew
His spirit from its body. His body could be committed
to the sepulchre in full confidence of resurrection. And
because of Him, all who believe in Him likewise "sorrow
not, even as others which have no hope. For if we believe
that Jesus died, and rose again, them also that sleep in
Jesus will God bring with Him" (I Thessalonians 4:13,
14).

*"Neither wilt thou suffer thine Holy One to see cor-
ruption."* Not only would His body not return to the
dust; it would not even begin the normal process of post-
mortal decay. It would simply "rest" in death until He
returned. In the meantime, for the three days His body
was in the grave, Christ was still alive in His spirit, "by
which he went and preached unto the spirits in prison;
which once were disobedient, when the longsuffering of
God waited in the days of Noah" (I Peter 3:19, 20). This
was not a preaching of the Gospel, but a proclaiming of

victory and judgment to those evil spiritual powers (the same ones of whom Peter also spoke in his second epistle — the "angels that sinned" and who were "cast down to hell" and were "to be reserved unto judgment" (II Peter 2:4), who had tried to thwart God's plan of redemption through corrupting all flesh in the original world before the Flood.) Following this visit to their great prison in the depths of the earth, He would return to His body waiting in the tomb, fashion it into an eternal body of glory, rise from the dead, and ascend to heaven. "Who is gone into heaven, and is on the right hand of God: angels and authorities and powers being made subject unto Him" (I Peter 3:22).

Furthermore, He would return with "the keys of Hades and of death" (Revelation 1:18), together with the spirits of all who had previously died in faith. "When He ascended up on high, He led captivity captive" after He had "also descended first into the lower parts of the earth" (Ephesians 4:8, 9).

If anyone should be inclined to reject the idea of a prison (or "hell" or "pit" — various terms are used in Scripture with essentially the same place under consideration) in the deep interior of the earth on the ground that geologists reject such a notion, he should remember that no geological instruments are capable of determining whether or not such a region exists, and thus no geologist or other scientist is capable of refuting the clear testimony of the Bible that it does exist.

Furthermore, if anyone is disposed to reject the bodily resurrection predicted there on the basis that this is scientifically impossible, let him realize that this is the very point. God, not the scientists, ordained those principles in nature which we now call laws of science. Miracles, therefore, are possible — in fact, a miracle could well be defined as an event that is impossible by the laws of science, but which happens nonetheless. The historic *fact* of the bodily resurrection of Christ meets all the objective criteria of historicity as well as or better than any other fact of history.

The final verse of Psalm 16 looks forward to His resurrection, ascension, and "session" at the right hand of His Father in heaven. *"Thou wilt show me the path of life."* Actually, the word "life" is in the plural, perhaps referring to the multitudes who have also received endless life through His mighty act. *"In thy presence, is fulness of joy."* Back in the presence of His Father, He would enter forever into the "joy that was set before Him" (Hebrews 12:2) as He prepared to drink the "cup" and "endure the cross." This was the joy of seeing God's purpose in creation finally accomplished, with multitudes of redeemed souls brought into God's presence and fellowship forever.

The psalm concludes with the magnificent testimony, *"At thy right hand there are pleasures forevermore."* This is the very first reference in the Bible to Christ's presence in heaven at the right hand of God, but far from the last. In all, there are 21 such references, and they can be arranged nicely into three groups of seven each.

The first such group consists of two references in the book of Psalms (the other being Psalm 110:1), and the five places in the New Testament that quote Psalm 110:1 (i.e., Matthew 22:44; Mark 12:36; Luke 20:42; Acts 2:34; Hebrews 20:42). Psalm 16:11 emphasizes the right hand of God as a place of fellowship, Psalm 110:1 as a source of power!

The second group consists of seven general references to Christ at God's right hand in Paul's epistles (Romans 8:34; Ephesians 1:20; Colossians 3:1; Hebrews 1:3; 8:1; 10:12; 12:2). The third group consists of seven references in other books of the New Testament (Matthew 26:64; Mark 14:62; 16:19; Luke 22: 69; Acts 7:55; 7:56; I Peter 3:22).

At the right hand of the Father there is, therefore, both full joy and eternal joy. No more sorrow, no more pain, no more tears, no more death! (Revelation 21:4). "If ye then be risen with Christ, seek those things which are above, where Christ sitteth on the right hand of God" (Colossians 3:1).

Chapter 14

CHRIST ON THE CROSS
(Psalm 22)

A thousand years before Christ, David wrote this re-markable poem of suffering and praise, taken in part from his own experience, but then going far beyond anything which he could ever have known in his own limited un-derstanding. The psalm constitutes a remarkable evi-dence of divine inspiration, as it outlines in minute prophetic detail the sufferings of Christ on the cross, as well as His victory over sin and the subsequent preaching of His gospel in all the world. As we shall see, there are aspects of the very structure of the psalm which still further confirm its divine inspiration.

The 22nd Psalm is quoted at least seven times in the New Testament, all in reference to Jesus Christ, so there is no doubt that it was understood by the Apostles as a Messianic psalm. It describes accurately the agony of death by crucifixion, in spite of the fact that this method of execution was virtually unknown at the time of David, es-pecially among the Jews. The reader is given an insight, not only into the physical sufferings of Christ, but also into the very thoughts of His heart. It is almost as though we were there ourselves with the soldiers and Pharisees around the cross, when "sitting down they watched Him there" (Matthew 27:36).

FORSAKEN BY THE FATHER
(Verses 1-5)

The psalm begins with the awful cry from the cross: "*My God, my God, why hast thou forsaken me*"? (see Matthew 27:46; Mark 15:34). Of the famous "seven words from the cross," this cry is the central "word," and the central word in this central "word" is the most important question ever to be answered: "*Why?*"

Why, indeed, should the pure and spotless Lamb be impaled on a cross to die? The queries continue in His soul: "*Why art thou so far from helping me*[!], *and from the words of my roaring*?"

The Lord Jesus was not, of course, *roaring* on the cross. He was utterly silent and, in some translations, the scholars have thought it more appropriate to say He was "groaning." Nevertheless, the Hebrew word really is "roaring," the same word as used for the roaring of a lion.

The clue to the answer to these questions is found later in the 32nd Psalm, written after David's sin in the matter of Bathsheba and Uriah. There David wrote: "When I kept silence, my bones waxed old through my roaring all the day long" (Psalm 32:3). David was silent on the outside, but "roaring" inwardly, because of the pressing guilt of his sin. The soul of the Lord Jesus likewise was roaring inwardly, because of the guilt of the sins of the whole world, which He was bearing in His own body on the tree (I Peter 2:24). His Father had turned His back on Him, as it were, because He was "of purer eyes than to behold evil," or to "look on iniquity" (Habakkuk 1:13).

He, who had always been in perfect communion with His Father, now was separated from Him because of sin. This, of course, is the essence of what hell will be (that is, complete separation from God). In those three terrible hours of darkness on the cross, Jesus Christ endured hell itself, in order to save sinners from the eternal separation from God (II Thessalonians 1:9) which they deserved.

Verse 2 of the psalm notes His suffering in the morning hours and then in "*the night season*," when the sun was darkened supernaturally in mid-day. The answer to His own question is given in verse 3. *"Thou art holy."* That is, the only possible reason that the Father could ever forsake His own beloved Son, is because He was made sin for us, and God's holiness requires that sin be judged.

And what a beautiful figure is Christ's testimony here (verse 3) of God's dwelling place, *"inhabiting the praises of Israel!"* He who would one day become the heir of all God's promises to Israel, even now could recall all God's promises and deliverances for His people, and how He had never failed when they called on Him. Yet God would not hear *Him*!

THE SCARLET WORM (Verse 6)

In verse 6, He is recorded to have said in His heart, *"But I am a Worm, and no man; a reproach of men, and despised of the people."* In Isaiah 52:14, it would be said prophetically that "His visage was so marred more than any man, and His form more than the sons of men." That is, from the awful beatings He endured in connection with His trial and crucifixion, He no longer even looked like a man. Isaiah 53:3 said, "He is despised and rejected of men."

These statements, however, hardly explain fully the identification of Himself as a worm. The key seems to lie in the recognition that this was a specific type of worm — the *scarlet worm.* As a matter of fact, the Hebrew word translated "worm" in this passage (*tolath*) is also frequently translated "scarlet" (e.g. Exodus 25:4) or "crimson" (Isaiah 1:18). The reason for this odd equivalence is because the scarlet worm was the source of a fluid from which the people of ancient times made their scarlet dyes.

Christ's portrayal of Himself as stained crimson on the cross thus immediately speaks to us in the words of Colossians 1:20. "Having made peace with the blood of His cross, by Him to reconcile all things unto Himself."

But no doubt the deeper significance of His identification of Himself as the Scarlet Worm lies in the re-

markable life-death cycle of this unique animal. For when
the mother worm of this species is ready to give birth to her
baby worms, she will emplant her body in a tree
somewhere, or a post, or a stick of wood, so firmly that she
can never leave again.

Then, when the young are brought forth, the mother's
body provides protection and sustenance for her young until they reach the stage where they can leave home and fend
for themselves. Then the mother dies. And as she dies, the
scarlet fluid in her body emerges to stain her body and the
bodies of her progeny and the wood of the tree where they
were given life by their dying mother.

What a picture of the blood-stained cross, and how "it
became Him, for whom are all things, and by whom are all
things, in bringing many sons unto glory, to make the cap-
tain of their salvation perfect through sufferings"
(Hebrews 2:10). Throughout the realm of the biological
kingdom, new life is always preceded by a time of travail
and possibly death, and this is always a divine portrait of
bringing forth sons to spiritual life through spiritual death.
Thus it is said prophetically of Christ, "He shall see of the
travail of His soul and shall be satisfied" (Isaiah 53:11).
Because of His death, not only are individual souls
delivered unto everlasting life through a "new birth," but
so ultimately "the creation itself will be delivered from the
bondage of corruption" at the "manifestation of the sons
of God" (Romans 8:19, 21). The redemption price was
great, but the result is endless joy and glory.

PRINCIPALITIES AND POWERS
(Verses 7-13)

Verses 7 through 21 of this 22nd Psalm comprise one of
the most remarkable passages ever written, describing in
intimate detail the events that would take place a thousand years later on Calvary. The events are told through
the eyes and heart of the One hanging on the "Tree"
planted there.

"All they that see me laugh me to scorn: they shoot out

the lip, they shake the head, saying, He trusted on the Lord
that He would deliver him; let Him deliver him, seeing He
delighted in him."

Instead of compassion for the innocent victim and sorrow over His suffering, there is nothing but gloating and
mocking. Listen to the record of its fulfillment: "And they
that passed by reviled Him, wagging their heads
. . . . Likewise also the chief priests mocking Him, with
the scribes and elders, said, He saved others; Himself He
cannot save . . . . He trusted in God; let Him deliver Him
now, if He will have Him; for He said, I am the Son of God"
(Matthew 27:39-43).

In the next two verses of the psalm, He recalls His unique
conception and birth, when He entered the world in
human flesh. "*Thou art He that took me out of the womb:*
Thou didst make me hope when I was upon my mother's
breasts." He had left His throne in heaven to take up
residence in a body "prepared" for Him (Hebrews 10:5) in
a virgin's womb, and He had been conscious of His Father's
presence and fellowship even when in the embryonic and
infant stages of the growth of that body. Throughout His
human pilgrimage, He knew that "He that sent me is with
me: the Father hath not left me alone; for I do always those
things that please Him" (John 8:29). Yet, finally, here
on the cross, He prays in anguish: "*Be not far from me;*
for trouble is near; for there is none to help." Even His
Father had apparently forsaken Him. Trouble, indeed,
was *very* near! A malevolent horde of the demonic hosts
of darkness surrounded Him, invisible to human eyes
but viciously real, anticipating imminent victory over
their age-long Enemy. "This was their hour, and the
power of darkness" (Luke 22:52). "That old Serpent"
(Revelation 12:9) was inflicting his violent sting of death
on the Seed of the Woman (Genesis 3:15), and like a
rabid menagerie of wild animals, his demonic spirits
were closing in for the kill. There were *"many bulls . . .*
strong bulls of Bashan" compassing Him. These wicked
bull-spirits had long ago corrupted the Canaanites in the
kingdom of Bashan, producing and possessing an evil

race of giants (note Genesis 6:4; Deuteronomy 3:1-12), which had been destroyed by the Israelites through the strength of their God. There, also, He could see that *"dogs have compassed me"* — perhaps referring to the vicious demons controlling the Gentile soldiers who had so cruelly scourged and mocked Him (verse 16). *"Unicorns"* were there also (a term referring to the mighty *aurochs,* long extinct, but of unexcelled ferocity when living), aptly symbolizing the other fierce spirits hovering over Him (verse 21). Furthermore, there were *"ravening and roaring lions"* — including Satan himself (I Peter 5:8) — *"gaping upon Him with their mouths"* (verse 13), and seeking to devour Him.

"The assembly of the wicked have enclosed me!" That evil congregation dancing around their victim (apostate priests and brutal soldiers, jeering rabble and hordes of invisible demonic powers) little realized that they were only securing their own eternal doom. A great transaction was there being effected, planned long before the foundation of the world.

"Blotting out the handwriting of ordinances that was against us, which was contrary to us, [He] took it out of the way, nailing it to His cross; and having spoiled principalities and powers, He made a show of them openly, triumphing over them in it" (Colossians 2:14, 15). "Forasmuch then as the children are partakers of flesh and blood, He also Himself likewise took part of the same; that through death, He might destroy him that had the power of death, that is, the devil; and deliver them who through fear of death were all their lifetime subject to bondage" (Hebrews 2:14, 15).

Though the Serpent had bruised His heel, He would crush the head of that wicked one, destroying him and all who followed him, whether man or angel, in everlasting fire (Matthew 25:41). The accomplishment of this great work, however, required that He must first satisfy the righteous justice of a holy God, in offering His own suffering and death in substitution for the deserved penalty of eternal death pronounced for the sins of the world. He must first "by the grace of God, taste death for every man" (Hebrews 2:9).

THE AGONY OF CRUCIFIXION
(Verses 14-18)

In verses 14 through 18 of Psalm 22 are described prophetically, a thousand years in advance, the details of the physical sufferings and indignities that Christ must endure in His crucifixion. *"I am poured out like water — all my bones are out of joint — my heart is like wax — melted in the midst of my bowels."* Suspended by spikes which *"pierced my hands and my feet,"* the unnatural strains forced His bones to tear out of their joints, the body to dehydrate, the heart eventually to collapse and rupture. Probably the most agonizingly painful form of execution ever invented by human cruelty, the hideous Cross will remain forever as the ultimate measure of man's wickedness and of God's love. Almost unnoticed as we view His awful sufferings is the remarkable evidence of divine inspiration which this psalm provides. The mathematical probability of David's being able to predict these events in such detail without the guidance of the Holy Spirit is, for all practical purposes, absolutely zero!

"My strength is dried up like a potsherd; and my tongue cleaveth to my jaws." Jesus had become like a dessicated piece of splintered clay, and the thirst was beyond imagination. Even the normal fluids of the mouth had dried away in the burning sun that had preceded the noonday darkness. *"Thou hast brought me into the dust of death."* Because of Adam's sin, all men must return to the dust, of course, but God had promised that the body of the second Adam would never see corruption (Psalm 16:10). He would enter and experience death, therefore, but its "dust" does not here refer to the destiny of His body. The term must refer rather to the enduring of every tiny element of suffering that anyone would ever have to endure.

THE CLIMAX OF SUFFERING
(Verses 19-21)

To the physical agonies, of course, were added the mental humiliations. The first Adam had been provided a coat of skins to cover his nakedness (Genesis 3:21). The last Adam had every garment stripped from Him, as He hung suspended before the leers of the carnal and bestial mob around Him. "*I may tell all my bones: they look and stare upon me.*"

The Scriptures mercifully spare both Him and us of any further chronicling of the obscene curses and physical torments inflicted on Him during the horrible hours on the cross. However, there is one remarkable incident which is mentioned. "*They part my garments among them, and cast lots upon my vesture*" (verse 18). This is almost the only specific event at the cross which is mentioned in all four of the Gospels (Matthew 27:35; Mark 15:24; Luke 23:34; John 19:23, 24). There must be a special reason why this one event is emphasized in this way.

So far as the record goes, these few items of clothing were the only personal possessions ever owned by the Lord Jesus Christ (Maker of heaven and earth!) during His life on earth. "Though He was rich, yet for your sakes He became poor" (II Corinthians 8:9). Though He has been "appointed heir of all things" (Hebrews 1:2), the only inheritance He left at His death was the "New Testament" and its "promise of eternal inheritance" (Hebrews 5:15).

And even His pitiful scraps of clothing were stolen and appropriated by His executioners, not allowing even those to be given to His grieving mother. What He had taught by precept, He also taught by example: "Lay not up for yourselves treasures upon earth" (Matthew 6:19). No doubt, there will be great embarrassment when we enter one day into His presence, as He asks us concerning the possessions that *we* have left upon earth!

In verses 19, 20, and 21, we have the climax of His prayer, at the very peak of His sufferings during the three hours of hell's darkness. In agony and urgency, He calls upon God to help Him before Satan's triumph is complete. He has endured all the sufferings of earth and hell, and it is unthinkable that the Son of God can die forever, with Satan usurping the throne of the universe.

"Deliver my soul from the sword: my darling from the power of the dog." The word for "darling" is, in the Septuagint, translated *monogenes* — the same word as in John 3:16 — "only begotten." The Father surely will not forever turn His back on His beloved Son, once the price for sin is paid.

"Save me from the lion's mouth — from the horns of the unicorns." Satan, the roaring lion, is about to devour Him, and the mighty bulls to impale Him. But, then, the Father's silence finally is broken! *"Thou hast heard me!"* (verse 21).

No more, from this verse on, is heard the roaring of the lions and the bellowing of the bulls, the barking dogs, or the hissing serpents, or the jeering and cursing of the blood-thirsty mob. The hour of darkness is past; the light has dawned. Satan is a defeated foe, and Christ "hath abolished death and brought life and immortality to light through the gospel" (II Timothy 1:10).

THE SONG OF PRAISE
(Verse 22)

There are several themes in these latter verses—resurrection, witnessing, victory — but probably the most important concept is that of praise. In fact, there is a very remarkable structural pattern that comes to the surface when we consider this theme of praise.

In a very real sense, the very reason for the unique phenomenon of *language* is in order that God might be able to communicate His will and His plans to men, and that men might in turn respond to God in *praise!* The ability of communicating in intelligible, abstract, symbolic vocabularies and phonologies is an ability shared equally by all tribes among mankind, but an ability which is completely absent among animals. The phenomenon of language has no evolutionary explanation — it is uniquely an attribute of the image of God in man. And the highest function of human language is to praise the Lord.

This book of Psalms is the longest book in the Bible and is uniquely a book of praise. In fact, it is commonly called the *Hallal* Book — the book of the "praises" of Israel. Furthermore, it has a unique structure. The other books of the Bible originally had no chapter and verse divisions — these were developed much later by medieval scholars as a matter of convenience. The chapter and verse divisions of the book of Psalms, however, were there right from the start. Each psalm comprises a chapter, and the verses correspond to the obvious poetic divisions.

It is also significant that the medium in which God first chose to communicate His eternal Word in written form to man was the Hebrew language. The Hebrew language in turn is built around an alphabet of 22 letters, so that this number (22) seems often associated in the Bible with both the written Word and the living Word, Jesus Christ. Christ, in fact, called Himself the "Alpha and Omega" (that is, the first and last letters of the Greek language in which the New Testament was written — see Revelation 22:13), thus emphasizing that He is, Himself, the very Word of God (John 1:1, 14).

Now, although the great theme of the book of Psalms is that of praise, it is remarkable that the verb "to praise" (Hebrew *hallal*) is never used in the first 21 of the psalms. The Holy Spirit seemingly refrained from using this word until it could first be recorded as coming from the lips of the suffering Savior, here in this 22nd Psalm.

It must be much more than coincidence, considering the fact that this number "22" represents both the Word and the very purpose of language, that it is found for the first time (at least in the book of Psalms) here in this 22nd verse of the 22nd Psalm! "I will declare thy name unto my brethren: in the midst of the congregation will I *praise* thee!" Right at the very pinnacle of His suffering, He sings out a great note of praise, for His Father had heard and delivered Him. He had not, after all, really "hid His face from Him," nor had He "abhorred the affliction" (verse 24); He had, indeed, heard His cry, and when the cup of suffering had been emptied, He hastened once again to His presence.

This 22nd verse is quoted in the book of Hebrews, in the very chapter to which we have already frequently referred in this exposition. But there it is rendered: "For both He that sanctifieth and they who are sanctified are all of one [i.e., of one Father]; for which cause He is not ashamed to call them brethren, saying, I will declare thy name unto my brethren, in the midst of the church will I sing praise unto thee" (Hebrews 2:11, 12).

The congregation in which He is the great "Song-Leader," the "Praise-Leader," is thus the church. The "assembly of the wicked" around Him had been routed, but there was left around the cross a very little flock — the remnants of that first church that He had established upon the Rock of His deity and the salvation He would provide through His blood (note Matthew 16:18; 18:17; Acts 20:28). It was in the midst of *that* congregation (John the beloved, his mother, and the other women) that He first offered up the sacrifice of praise, but since that day, "where two or three are gathered together in my name, there am I in the midst of them" (Matthew 18:20). In His prayer the previous night in the upper room, He had said, "I have manifested thy name unto the men which thou gavest me out of the world" (John 17:6). That name was "Father," and He was not ashamed to call them His "brethren."

THE VICTORY AND THE COMMISSION
(Verses 23-31)

At verse 23, there is a change of person. In the first 22 verses the entire psalm is a prayer, with the one on the cross praying to His God and Father, the pronouns "I" and "thee" appearing almost continuously. At this point, however, the psalm becomes an exhortation to its readers. The Holy Spirit Himself, through David, speaks of Christ in the third person and directly to His readers in the second person.

The theme thus now turns sharply from one of suffering to one of praise. Christ first offered praise because of victory over death and Satan. Now we may continually (Hebrews 13:15) offer the sacrifice of praise, giving thanks to Him for His great love for us. "Ye that fear the Lord, praise Him! — glorify Him! — fear Him!"

Then comes the natural response to this great exhortation, in verse 25: *"My praise shall be of thee in the great congregation: I will pay my vows before them that fear Him."* This is the testimony of the redeemed. As the Lord even now leads our praises in each little congregation, so we shall all one day share our testimonies in that great congregation, as we enter "the city of the living God, the heavenly Jerusalem, and to an innumerable company of angels, to the general assembly and church of the firstborn, which are written in heaven, and to God the judge of all, and to the spirits of just men made perfect, and to Jesus the mediator of the new covenant" (Hebrews 12:21-23).

And in that great day, *"the meek shall eat and be satisfied: they shall praise the Lord that seek Him: your heart shall live forever. All the ends of the world shall remember and turn unto the Lord: and all the kindreds of the nations shall worship before thee. For the kingdom is the Lord's and He is the governor among the nations"* (verses 26-28). In these verses are summed up all the great prophecies and promises of all the ages, when God's great purposes in creation will have finally been accomplished. Every knee shall bow and every tongue shall confess that the Lamb who was on the altar is the King on the eternal throne. Both those that prosper (*"the fat upon earth"*) and those who die (*"all they that go down to the dust"*) shall bow down to Him. Though *"none can keep alive his own soul,"* we shall forever thank Him for the travail through which He passed in order to keep our souls alive through the endless ages.

In the meantime, we that have been thus "born again" through receiving His life by faith comprise "*a seed that shall serve Him"* (verse 30). Remember again the scarlet worm and the many sons brought forth through suffering. This innumerable spiritual progeny will continue serving Him until the coming day when He will be recognized as governor among the nations. The latter part of verse 30 says literally: *"This shall be accounted of the Lord for a generation."* That is, each succeeding generation would continue recounting the same old, but always new, story of the great love of the One who had died to bring life. "One generation shall praise thy works to another, and shall declare thy mighty acts" (Psalm 145:4).

This is the final refrain of Psalm 22. *"They shall come and declare His righteousness unto a people that shall be born, that He hath done this!"*

This very last phrase is, literally, "He hath finished!" The mighty act which the Scarlet One had been about ever since He left the presence of His Father in glory, to be *"cast upon Him from the womb"* (verse 10), culminating in the cross has been accomplished. The victory cry, "It is finished!" still echoes through the centuries and provides continuing comfort and counsel for the seed that serves Him.

Chapter 15

THE GOOD SHEPHERD WITH HIS SHEEP
(Psalm 23)

Although the 23rd Psalm is one of the Bible's shortest chapters, its six verses contain many evidences of divine inspiration, in terms of both its interesting numeric structure and also its wonderful message. It is quite likely the best-loved chapter in the Bible, one of the first learned by Sunday School children and the last requested for death-bed reading by dying Christians. It was written by David, and its shepherd-theme no doubt grew out of his own experiences as a shepherd boy, but its message far transcends anything that could be devised by David or any other man, speaking with great power and blessing to all people of every time and place.

The psalm's shepherd, of course, is none other than the Lord Jesus Christ. He frequently spoke of Himself as the shepherd (John 10:14; Matthew 25:32; 26:31, etc.). He called Himself the good shepherd, dying for His sheep (John 10:11); Paul spoke of Him as the great shepherd, guiding His sheep (Hebrews 13:20, 21); and Peter saw Him as the chief shepherd, rewarding His sheep (I Peter 5:4).

The psalm also refers to Him as the Lord (i.e., *Jehovah*). This Old Testament name of God has been appropriated and applied to Christ in the New Testament — for example, Acts 2:21, 36, quoting Joel 2:31. Thus "Jehovah my Shepherd" in Psalm 23:1 is to be understood as none other than Jesus Christ.

THE REMARKABLE STRUCTURE
OF THE TWENTY-THIRD PSALM

Psalm 23 is probably the greatest testimony to the believer's security to be found in the Bible, at least in the Old Testament. This theme of security is woven into the very structure of the psalm.

All six verses are intensely subjective, with the writer opening his deepest heart in his expressions about, and to, the Lord. There is beautiful symmetry in the respective verse themes, which can be summarized as follows:

Verse one.	Statement of Faith in the Present
Verse two.	Testimony of God's Faithfulness
Verse three.	Testimony of God's Faithfulness
Verse four.	Prayer of Thanksgiving
Verse five.	Prayer of Thanksgiving
Verse six.	Statement of Faith for the Future

These themes are accompanied by twelve references to the Lord, organized symmetrically as follows:

Verse one.	"The Lord" (once)
Verse two.	"He" (twice)
Verse three.	"He" (thrice)
Verse four.	"Thou" (thrice)
Verse five.	"Thou" (twice)
Verse six.	"The Lord" (once)

It seems obvious that this remarkable arrangement could not be attributed to chance, and almost as unlikely that David contrived it. It can best be explained by inspiration of the Holy Spirit. Six is a number usually associated with human weakness and incompleteness, but the number twelve seems always associated with God's special provision for mankind in calling and organizing chosen servants for dealing with the spiritual needs of His people.

Note also that there are no less than 17 references in

the psalm to the believer himself, through use of the first person pronouns ("I," "me," "my," etc.), and this number commonly is peculiarly connected with the doctrine of assurance and security in Christ. For example, there are 17 categories of opposition to the Christian listed in Romans 8:35-39 which can *never* "separate us from the love of God which is in Christ Jesus, our Lord." The Ark of safety which carried believers through the awful judgment of the cataclysmic deluge rested "on the seventeenth day of the month" after the flood had come on "the seventeenth day of the month" five months earlier (Genesis 8:4; 7:11 — the first mention of 17 in the Bible).

In John 21:11 there were "153 great fishes" brought to shore by the disciples in a net which did not break, symbolically representing those believers in all nations who would be won to Christ through the witnessing of those "fishers of men" whom Christ would send forth into all the world and who would be brought safely to shore in the gospel net. The number 153 seems to have been particularly mentioned because it is the sum of all the numbers 1 through 17 and the product of 9 by 17. The sum of its digits (1+5+3) equals the other factor 9, while the sum of the cubes of its digits again equals 153.

But while such mathematical features are interesting, and while they provide incidental evidences of divine origin of the psalm's structure, it is the message of the words themselves which brings blessing and the assurance of salvation and security to the heart of the believer.

ALL NEEDS SUPPLIED BY CHRIST
(Verse 1)

In each of the last five verses of Psalm 23 two vital needs are mentioned, needs shared by all men but probably felt most keenly by the believing Christian who, like a lost sheep in a dangerous country, is living in a world which is at enmity with God. He desperately needs care and direction which he himself cannot provide, just as the sheep needs the shepherd.

Verse one simply contains the comforting assurance that all these needs will be supplied. *"The Lord is my shepherd."* Jehovah is the great covenant and redemptive name of God, and the expression here is actually a compound name — "Jehovah my Shepherd." The immediate conclusion that necessarily follows is: *"I cannot lack!"* A human shepherd may occasionally be careless or ineffective, but not Jehovah. "My God shall supply all your need according to His riches in glory by Christ Jesus" (Philippians 4:19).

REST AND PEACE
(Verse 2)

The first need is rest. God rested from His great work of creation, and the lost sinner needs to find rest for his own soul. He has attempted unsuccessfully to find rest in his own way and to provide his own needs. A great burden is lifted when he finally places complete trust in the Shepherd. "There remaineth therefore a rest to the people of God. For he that is entered into his rest, he also hath ceased from his own works, as God did from His" (Hebrews 4:9, 10).

That rest is symbolized here in Psalm 23:2 by the resting in *"grassy* pastures." The phrase *"maketh me to lie down"* is one word in the Hebrew and does not intend to indicate a forced rest, but rather can be expressed as "causeth me to rest."

The Christian may not often be able to rest physically, but even in the midst of great physical or mental toil as he serves the Lord, he does again and again lie down in great ease spiritually in God's green, grassy meadows, in living fellowship with the Lord.

And the Lord also gives great peace! He "leadeth me" means "gently guideth me." The "still waters" are not stagnant waters, but "stilled waters," waters that have been brought to rest by the Lord's power. Even though the great storm may almost overwhelm us, He says, "Peace, be still" (Mark 4:39), and we find peace in the midst of turmoil. "Your strength is to sit still," God told the fearful Israelites; "in returning and rest shall ye be saved; in quietness and confidence shall be your strength" (Isaiah 30:7, 15). The Lord is well in control of every situation, and our peace is simply to be where He is!

HEALTH AND GUIDANCE
(Verse 3)

"*He restoreth my soul*" means literally,"bringeth back life." Genuine health is one of God's choice provisions for His people. Rest and peace are, in themselves, the best medicines. "Trust in the Lord with all thine heart; and lean not unto thine own understanding. In all thy ways acknowledge Him, and He shall direct thy paths. Be not wise in thine own eyes: fear the Lord, and depart from evil. It shall be health to thy navel, and marrow to thy bones" (Proverbs 3:5-8).

The Christian normally does not need to worry overmuch about what he eats (Matthew 6:25; I Timothy 4:4; Romans 14:17) or what exercise he gets (I Timothy 4:8), as long as He is placing God's will and His kingdom first (Matthew 6:33). God, of course, is able to heal our diseases in answer to prayer if it is His will, but even if we have a "thorn in the flesh" which He elects not to remove, we always have His gracious assurance: "My grace is sufficient for thee: for my strength is made perfect in weakness" (II Corinthians 11:7-10).

One of our greatest needs, of course, is to know His will. And so, He also provides guidance. When the psalmist says in this verse, "*He leadeth me,*" it is a different word from that in verse 2. There, "He gently guides me"; here, "He forcibly guides me." If we stray out of His will, that is, He will constrain us back into the "*paths* [literally 'tracks'] *of righteousness.*" "The steps of a good man are ordered by the Lord; and He delighteth in his way. Though he fall, he shall not be utterly cast down: for the Lord upholdeth him with His hand" (Psalm 37:23, 24). All of this is for our good (Romans 8:28; Hebrews 12:11), but even more, it is *"for His name's sake."* That He will show us His will (through His word, through circumstances, through inner conviction) without the necessity of falling and being chastised, if we are really willing to follow it, is obvious from such Scriptures as John 7:17; Romans 12:1, 2; and others.

COURAGE AND COMFORT
(Verse 4)

If we are in His will, we need not fear either man or devil. The word *"evil"* in this verse can refer to evil men, evil phenomena, to dangers of any kind. Even *"the shadow of death"* (one word in the original connoting "the nearness of death") need generate no fears in the believer. God can deliver us either from death, or through death, depending on His will, and since "to live is Christ, to die is gain" (Philippians 1:21), we are victors in either case! The dark "valley of weeping" can be transformed into a flowing well (Psalm 84:6) of living water.

"Thy rod" (literally "thy club" or "thy sceptre") and *"thy staff"* (literally "thy cane" or "thy crook") suffice either to force us back or pull us back, as need may dictate, into the right tracks. This might seem at first a strange way of bringing *"comfort,"* until one notes that the same word also means "repent." God's chastenings and corrections are calculated to bring us to repentance, and we have here His gracious assurance that we, as His sheep, will never be allowed to be comfortable when out of His will.

PROTECTION AND PROVISION
(Verse 5)

There are enemies all around the believer in this world, both human and demonic, but He provides all our needs right in the very *"presence of our enemies,"* and they are powerless to prevent it. "The angel of the Lord encampeth round about them that fear Him, and delivereth them"

(Psalm 34:7). "And the Lord shall deliver me from every evil work, and will preserve me unto His heavenly kingdom" (II Timothy 4:18).

"Thou anointest my head with oil; my cup runneth over." The word "anoint" here is actually "fatten." Not only will the Shepherd protect the sheep from the enemies surrounding him, but also He will fatten (greatly bless and prosper) him, beyond measure, to God's glory and his enemies' discomfiture.

LOVE AND LIFE
(Verse 6)

All this and heaven, too! Not only does the believer have rest and peace, health and guidance, courage and comfort, protection and provision, in Christ, He also has the promise of His unfailing love throughout this life and the endless life to come.

God's *"goodness and mercy* [literally 'loving-kindness'] *will follow him all the days of his* [earthly] *life."* The word "follow" is a strong word, meaning "chase after." In addition to "leading me" (verses 2 and 3), He will pursue after me, like the great hound of heaven, never allowing retreat or escape. "Whither shall I go from thy spirit? or whither shall I flee from thy presence? If I ascend up into heaven, thou art there: if I make my bed in hell, behold, thou art there. If I take the wings of the morning, and dwell in the uttermost parts of the sea; Even there shall thy hand lead me, and thy right hand shall hold me" (Psalm 139:7-10).

Then, when this life is over, the believer *"will dwell"* with the Lord and His people *"forever."* The *"house of the Lord"* means "the family of the Lord" (like "the house of David," etc.; note Ephesians 2:19-22; Revelation 21:2, 3). "In the ages to come" (Ephesians 2:7), we will enjoy the fellowship of all the redeemed, as well as the Lord Himself.

Listen again to the Lord Jesus: "My sheep hear my voice, and I know them, and they follow me: And I give unto them eternal life; and they shall never perish, neither shall any man pluck them out of my hand" (John 10:28, 29).

Chapter 16

THE INCARNATION AND VIRGIN BIRTH
(Psalm 40)

THE CHRISTMAS PSALM

The true testimony of Christmas, at least to the Christian, is the incarnation. When Christ came into the world — that is, when God became man — the age-long barrier between earth and heaven was finally crossed. This grand theme, along with the great work of salvation He came to accomplish, is the message of the 40th Psalm.

Although the psalm was written by David and is in the first person, it is clear from the New Testament references to it that the person speaking is actually the Lord Jesus Christ Himself. The context, furthermore, indicates that most likely it represents the inward meditation of His heart, as He hung on the cross dying for the sin of the world. In this respect, it is a corollary of Psalm 22, which likewise reveals His thoughts during the hours of His darkest sufferings, when even His heavenly Father had forsaken Him (Psalm 22:1; Matthew 27:46).

The 40th Psalm seems probably to contain His testimony during the interval following the three hours of darkness on the cross, but before His actual physical demise. No longer was He separated from His Father

(Luke 23:46); the actual experience of hell (separation from God) was "finished" (John 19:30). All that remained was for Him, in the Spirit, to proclaim His victory to the wicked spirits in the heart of the earth (I Peter 3:18, 19; Matthew 12:40); to set the captives free (Isaiah 61:1; Ephesians 4:8-10); and to return to His own body resting in death in the tomb with the very keys to death and hell, alive forevermore (Revelaton 1:18).

TESTIMONY OF DELIVERANCE
(Verses 1-5)

In His testimony, as recorded in Psalm 40, He expresses thankfulness for the great deliverance already experienced and continues to pray for the full accomplishment of God's purpose in His sufferings. With this context in mind, let us now take a verse-by-verse journey through this marvelous psalm.

1. *"I waited patiently for the Lord: and he inclined unto me, and heard my cry."* The Scripture admonishes: "For ye have need of patience, that, after ye have done the will of God, ye might receive the promise" (Hebrews 10:36). He had come to do God's will (verse 8) and had finally accomplished it. For three long hours, especially, He had endured Hell itself, suffering patiently what others deserved to suffer, but from which they could now be freed. Finally, He uttered the sad cry of desolation and God heard and answered.

2. *"He brought me up also out of an horrible pit, out of the miry clay, and set my feet upon a rock, and established my goings."* When God heard, then He lifted His soul out of the darkness. All others who had died had been forced to confinement in the great abyss of Hades, the horrible pit in the depths of the earth (the fact that men ridicule the idea of such a prison enclosure far down in the earth's core does not prove it is not there; there is ample room, and no seismic instruments yet developed can determine otherwise). Even those who

had died in faith were there, because no efficacious offering, which would purge their sins, had yet been made. But *He* could not be bound there! "For thou wilt not leave my soul in hell" (Psalm 16:10). Otherwise, "what profit is there in my blood when I go down to the pit?" (Psalm 30:9).

3. *"And He hath put a new song in my mouth, even praise unto our God; many shall see it, and fear, and shall trust in the Lord."* The glorious "song of the Lamb" (Revelation 15:3, 4), which we shall hear in His presence one day, is such a testimony of praise: "Great and marvelous are thy works, Lord God Almighty, just and true are thy ways, thou King of saints." The message of salvation which His great work releases has led multitudes to trust in the Lord, everyone testifying in his own turn that he also has been delivered from the miry clay and his path established on the solid rock. "Upon this Rock I will build my church," He said, "and the gates of hell shall not prevail against it" (Matthew 16:18).

4. *"Blessed is that man that maketh the Lord his trust, and respecteth not the proud, nor such as turn aside to lies."* This is both a personal testimony on the part of Jesus and a promise to all others. He, as the perfect Man, the second Adam, had resisted Satan, the proud one (Isaiah 14:12-14; Ezekiel 28:17) and the father of lies (John 8:44). "He that committeth sin is of the devil," but "in Him is no sin" (I John 3:5, 8). Though he could not deceive Jesus, even in the physical weakness of His humanity (Matthew 4:10), Satan continues to this very hour as the deceiver of the whole world (Revelation 12:9), seeking to turn men away from "the true God and eternal life" (I John 5:19,20). Yet, "blessed are all they that put their trust in Him" (Psalm 2:12).

5. *"Many, O Lord my God, are thy wonderful works which thou hast done, and thy thoughts which are to usward: they cannot be reckoned up in order unto thee: if I would declare and speak of them, they are more than can be numbered."* Even in the midst of His sufferings

on the cross, the Lord Jesus could continually meditate on both the works and the words of the infinite God. This testimony, no doubt, includes God's works in creation as well as those in salvation. Every system in nature — even the most insignificant microorganisms, and even the very structure of matter itself — provides further insight to the thoughts of their Creator. All are marvels of design, so that even the study of science is nothing but "thinking God's thoughts after Him," as some of the greatest scientists have testified. Even greater are His redemptive works. "O the depth of the riches both of the wisdom and knowledge of God!. . . . For of Him, and through Him, and to Him are all things: to whom be glory forever" (Romans 11:33, 36).

THE PREPARED BODY
(Verses 6-8)

6. *"Sacrifice and offering thou didst not desire: mine ears hast thou opened: burnt offering and sin offering hast thou not required."* We now enter the very heart of the psalm, as well as that of the Savior, as He rehearses the reason for His incarnation. Not any of the four great offerings and sacrifices of the Levitical system — the "sacrifice" (that is, the "peace offering" of Leviticus 3) or the "offering" (that is, the "meal offering" of Leviticus 2) or the "burnt offering" (Leviticus 1) or the "sin offering" (Leviticus 4) — were either desired or required by God as true sacrifices for sin. They could only, as evidence of the offeror's faith, serve as a temporary atonement (literally "covering") for sin, but they could never really "take away sins" (Hebrews 10:4).

For this a greater sacrifice was required — "the Lamb of God, which taketh away the sin of the world" (John 1:29). But before He could take away the sin of the world, He would have to come into the world. Though He had created man, He must Himself *become* man, then die for man, in order to save man from his sins. And for this, the Son of God must declare to His Father His willingness to become the Son of Man.

This He did, in token whereof "mine ears hast thou opened." The symbolism of this remarkable action speaks of complete submission of one's body to do the will of his master. When an indentured servant in ancient Israel was due to be set free following his term of service, he could instead make the decision to remain in servitude forever, if he so chose. In token of this decision, "his master shall bore his ear through with an awl; and he shall serve him forever" (Exodus 21:6). The meaning of this ritual was apparently the complete submission of the servant's ear to the voice of his master. Whatever his master commanded, his servant would do forthwith. The Son thus completely yielded himself to do the will of His Father, and this will required Him to become man.

This is the passage quoted in the New Testament which definitely identifies the 40th Psalm as Messianic. Remarkably, however, the Holy Spirit used the Septuagint translation, which renders the clause by "a body hast thou prepared me" (Hebrews 10:5). The opening of the ear, by divine inspiration, is thus in this case interpreted as synonymous with taking on a specially prepared human body. Thus, the verse speaks of the unique work of incarnation, when God became man. "The word was made flesh, and dwelt among us" (John 1:14).

7. *"Then said I, Lo, I come; in the volume of the book it is written of me."* After submitting Himself to the will of the Father in this way, the Son proceeded to come to earth. The testimony recorded here must have been given prior to His coming to earth, but it had been written down in the volume of the book even before that. Both the book of God's Word (note Psalm 119:89, 160 "thy word forever settled in heaven" and "thy word true from the beginning") and the "book of life" (see Revelation 13:8) containing the names of the redeemed were written before the foundation of the world. God the Creator does not have "second thoughts" or "after thoughts"!

But exactly how could such a remarkable transition be accomplished? How could God become man — and, especially how could God become man without ceasing to be God? Man, ever since the Fall, has been in sin from his very birth. "Behold, I was shapen in iniquity, and in sin did my mother conceive me" (Psalm 51:5). If He were *only* man, then how could He save man?

These mysteries are resolved in the miracle of the virgin birth. "A body hast thou prepared me" (Hebrews 10:5, referring to His coming into the world). He did not enter the world at the time of the virgin birth, of course, but nine months earlier, at the time of His miraculous conception in the womb of the virgin Mary. The remarkable nature of this "preparation" of His body by God is pointed up by the fact that the same Greek word is used in the next chapter of Hebrews to tell how God created the universe — "the worlds were *framed* by the word of God" (Hebrews 11:3).

Such a body must be fully human and so must be formed from the elements of the earth as Adam's body had been (Genesis 2:7), but it must also be free of inherent sin or genetic defects, as Adam's body had been originally. He must "in all things . . . . be made like unto His brethren" (Hebrews 2:17) and be "in all points tested like as we are, yet without sin" (Hebrews 4:15). Though He could receive no genetic inheritance from His earthly parents or ancestors (otherwise, there would be no nonmiraculous way in which He would not likewise have inherited both the sin nature and its accompanying genetic defects from both his human parents), yet He must also be of the "seed of the woman" (Genesis 3:15), the "seed of Abraham" (Hebrews 2:16), and the "seed of David" (Romans 1:3). These Biblical requirements could only be met by a perfect human body supernaturally "framed" by God and placed as a single living cell (equivalent to the cell normally formed by the penetration of the "egg" of a woman by a male "seed") in the womb of a virgin descended from Abraham and David. In His growth from this one-celled stage, He would then share in all the experiences of mankind, from conception to death, yet be (as was the first Adam) without inherent sin.

8. "*I delight to do thy will, O my God; yea, thy law is within my heart.*" As the Son left the Father's home in heaven and took up a new residence ("*tabernacled* among us" — John 1:14) in the body God had prepared for Him, He set forth to do the Father's will, even though that will included the cross. God's law was in His heart, a condition yet future for other men (Hebrews 8:10).

RESULTS OF THE INCARNATION
(Verses 9-17)

9. "*I have preached righteousness in the great congregation: I have not refrained my lips, O Lord, thou knowest.*" Continuing His meditation there on the cross, the Savior recalled His ministry, preaching God's Word to God's people — not only in the land of Israel, but also anticipating in the Spirit His future preaching throughout the world throughout the ages. As He had prayed the night before, "I have given them thy word" (John 17:14). There is also mention of this "great congregation" in Psalm 22:25, in the same connection, but looking to the future. Quite possibly it includes not only the believers of all ages, but even the holy angels (Hebrews 12:23).

10. "*I have not hid thy righteousness within my heart; I have declared thy faithfulness and thy salvation: I have not concealed thy lovingkindness and thy truth from the great congregation.*" No man has seen God at any time, but the Son has declared Him. Note all the magnificent attributes of God which Christ revealed: "thy righteousness, thy faithfulness, thy salvation, thy lovingkindness, thy truth," also "thy will, thy law" (verse 8), "thy tender mercies" (verse 11). What an array of testimonies! Not only had Christ told of God in word; He had Himself displayed the attributes of God in person. "In Him dwells all the fulness of the Godhead

bodily" (Colossians 2:9).

11. *"Withhold not thou thy tender mercies from me, O Lord: let thy lovingkindness and thy truth continually preserve me."* In His perfect humanity, the Lord Jesus fully exhibited the life of prayer and trust in God that pleases Him and serves as an example for us. Even in the midst of excruciating pain and suffering, and facing imminent physical death, He trusted the overshadowing mercy and love of His Father.

12. *"For innumerable evils have compassed me about: mine iniquities have taken hold upon me, so that I am not able to look up; they are more than the hairs of mine head: therefore my heart faileth me."* Surrounding him there at the cross was a great host of wicked spirits — the "assembly of the wicked" (Psalm 22:16), the "principalities and powers" of darkness over whom He would soon triumph in His death (Colossians 2:15). Not only so, but the sins of all the world were laid upon Him, and His "iniquities" (literally, "punishments") were so heavy and so many that His head began to sink and His heart to break. That perfect, sinless body which had been prepared for Him by God when He came into the world was now unspeakably bruised and disfigured as He was about to leave the world. "His visage was so marred more than any man" (Isaiah 52:15). "But He was wounded for our transgressions, He was bruised for our iniquities; the chastisement of our peace was upon Him, and with His stripes we are healed" (Isaiah 53:5). "Who His own self bare our sins in His own body on the tree" (I Peter 2:24). Our key passage in the tenth chapter of Hebrews says that He had come into the world to do God's will through that prepared body, "by the which will we are sanctified through the offering of the body of Jesus Christ once for all" (Hebrews 10:10).

13. *"Be pleased, O Lord, to deliver me: O Lord, make haste to help me."* In His closing moments of life, the dying Savior prayed to the Father for His presence through death and the work yet to be accomplished. His body must be delivered from the wicked ones surrounding

Him (and indeed, God shortly sent the loving hands of Joseph and Nicodemus to care for that body and place it in Joseph's new tomb).

14. *"Let them be ashamed together that seek after my soul to destroy it; let them be driven backward and put to shame that wish me evil."* This prayer also was soon answered. Satan and his hosts of evil were there and no doubt believed they were gaining a great victory as they contrived to destroy His soul. But it was this very death that sealed their shame and doom forever! "Blotting out the handwriting of ordinances that was against us, which was contrary to us, and took it out of the way, nailing it to His cross; and having spoiled principalities and powers, He made a show of them openly, triumphing over them in it" (Colossians 2:14, 15). ". . . that through death He might destroy him that had the power of death, that is, the devil; and deliver them who through fear of death were all their lifetime subject to bondage" (Hebrews 2:15).

15. *"Let them be desolate for a reward of their shame that say unto me, Aha, aha."* This exclamation of His enemies is a Hebrew expression of malicious joy, with no real English equivalent. Those who take such delight in iniquity and, especially, in the suffering of the righteous, are at last to receive their equitable reward. They will be consigned finally to "shame and everlasting contempt" (Daniel 12:2).

16. *"Let all those that seek thee rejoice and be glad in thee: let such as love thy salvation say continually, the Lord be magnified."* In contrast to the unbelieving, whether men or demons, those whose hearts are right toward God may now be satisfied and full of joy, world without end. The word "salvation" is the Hebrew *yeshuah*, essentially the same as the human name given Him when God became man. This verse could even be read: "Let such as love thy Jesus say continually, the Lord be magnified." The promise of Christmas is fulfilled in the cross! No wonder the holy angels announcing His birth spoke of tidings of great joy. "But this

Man, after He had offered one sacrifice for sins forever, sat down on the right hand of God" (Hebrews 10:12).

17. *"But I am poor and needy: yet the Lord thinketh upon me: thou art my help and my deliverer: make no tarrying, O my God."* No matter how weak and helpless one may be, the Lord knows and cares. We may freely "cast all our cares upon Him" (I Peter 5:7), for He never will leave us or forsake us. If that be true, He would surely not be deaf to the prayers of His Holy One. The suffering for sin was over; He would now enter into the joy set before Him. In verse 13 was recorded His prayer for deliverance and help. In this final verse, he testified: "Thou *art* my help and deliverer." His prayer was answered. He who had waited in infinite patience as He had done the will of God (verse 1; compare Hebrews 10:36) was now ready to receive the promise fulfilled.

And so shall we! "For yet a little while, and He that shall come will come, and will not tarry" (Hebrews 10:37).

Chapter 17

THE WORD FOREVER

(Psalm 119)

INTRODUCTION

In many ways, the 119th Psalm is one of the most remarkable chapters in the Bible. With 176 verses, it is by far the longest chapter in the Bible. It is almost the middle chapter, but the central chapter is actually the shortest chapter, the two-verse long 117th Psalm. The middle verse of the Bible is Psalm 118:8 — "It is better to trust in the Lord than to put confidence in man."

But the most striking feature of the psalm is its constant emphasis on God's written word, the holy Scriptures. Practically every verse is a testimony to the value of the Scriptures, a fact which is all the more remarkable since the writer of the psalm had only a small portion of the complete Bible available in his day. If the Scriptures were such a blessing to him, how much more should they be so to us!

The 119th Psalm is of unknown authorship, one of the fifty anonymous psalms in the book of Psalms. Its real author, of course, is the Holy Spirit, and there is probably no chapter in the Bible containing more clear internal evidences of divine inspiration than this one.

NUMERICAL STRUCTURE

All of God's physical creation is filled with evidences of design and order, capable of being described and analyzed mathematically. It is not too surprising, then, that His written revelation (which is far superior to His revelation in nature) should likewise exhibit evidences of order and structure. Occasionally these are actually in the form of numerical patterns, and this is especially true in Psalm 119.

The most obvious numerical pattern is the psalmist's division into 22 stanzas of 8 verses each. Each of the 22 stanzas is headed by one of the 22 letters of the Hebrew alphabet. In the original Hebrew, the psalm is a remarkable acrostic, with the first letter of each verse consisting of the letter corresponding to its stanza. Thus, each of the first eight verses begin with the Hebrew letter *aleph,* each of the second eight with *beth,* the third eight with *gimel,* and so on.

It was the Hebrew language, of course, in which God chose to convey His Word to mankind originally, and it is appropriate that this unique psalm of the Word should be structured so strikingly around the Hebrew alphabet. The New Testament revelation was given in the Greek language and it is significant that He who is the living Word said in His last revelation, "I am Alpha and Omega" (Revelation 1:8; 22:13). Alpha and omega, of course, are the first and last letters of the Greek alphabet, and this claim of the Lord Jesus identifies Him as the very author of all language. In fact, the gift of language is a unique gift of God to man, not shared in any degree by animals, and completely inexplicable on any kind of evolutionary basis. Evidently the very purpose of language is to enable God to reveal Himself and His will to men, and for men to respond in praise to God.

It is not so immediately obvious why each stanza of the psalm has eight verses, but this also is singularly appropriate. The number 8 in the Bible is symbolic of resurrection and eternal life, and it is the living Word who gives eternal life through the written Word. "Being born again, not of corruptible seed, but of incorruptible, by the word of God, which liveth and abideth forever" (I Peter 1:23).

It is universally acknowledged that the number 7 in the Bible represents completeness and rest. The week of seven days regularly commemorates God's primeval week of creation. By the same token, the number 6 represents incompleteness and the number 8 represents a new beginning. Man was created on the 6th day, and always "comes short of the glory of God" in his sin and rebellion, so that 6 seems in the Bible commonly associated with man as separated from God. Conversely, 8 represents the perfect man, Jesus Christ, especially in His resurrected state, and thus also all who have received new life through faith in Him.

Christ was raised from the dead on the "eighth" day, the first day of a new week, after He had rested in the tomb on the sabbath day. It is significant that there are eight other specific "resuscitations" (not true resurrections, since these all died again later) mentioned in the Bible (three in the ministry of Elijah and Elisha — I Kings 17:22; II Kings 4:34, 35; 13:21; three in the ministry of Jesus — Matthew 9:24, 25; Luke 7:15; John 11:44; and two in the ministry of the apostles — Acts 9:40, 41; 20:9-12).

In the 119th Psalm, it is striking that there are exactly eight different words which are used to refer to the Scriptures. The number of occurrences of each forms the following pattern:

Torah (= "law")	25	19	*Imrah* (= "word")
Edah (= "testimony")	23	21	*Mishpat* (= "judgment")
Dabar (= "word")	23	21	*Piqqud* (= "precept")
Chuggah (= "statute")	22	22	*Mitzvah* (= "commandment")

Sum of each pair of most and least frequent occurrences = 44

Total occurrences = 4 × 44 = number of verses in
the psalm = 176

The above arrangement could hardly have been
deliberately contrived by the writer, and yet it is far too
regular and symmetrical to have occurred by chance.
The verbal inspiration of the Scriptures by the Holy
Spirit is the most satisfying explanation. It is interesting
that six verses in the psalm (3, 37, 90, 91, 122, 132) contain *no* reference to the Scriptures, but six verses contain
two references to the Scriptures (16, 43, 48, 160, 172).

But that is not all. It is well known that numbers in
both the Hebrew and Greek languages were expressed by
letters in the alphabet, each letter representing also a
certain number. The Jews and Greeks did not use
unique symbols such as the Arabic numerals which we
today use with the English language. Therefore, each
Hebrew and Greek word also had a distinct "numerical
value," which was simply the total of the numbers represented by the letters of the alphabet used in the word.

This is the plain literal meaning of the admonition in
Revelation 13:18 to "count the number of his name" —
that is, "add up the numerical values of the letters used
in his name." The name of this coming Beast, the man
of sin, will have a numerical value (when transliterated
into the New Testament Greek language, evidently) of
666, which is "the number of a man," and which will
enable those believers in that day who "have wisdom" to
identify him before he is openly revealed.

About one in every 10,000 names will have the
numerical value of 666, but presumably there will be
only one important political leader in that day with this
identification. The significant point about this in connection with Psalm 119, however, is that the name
"Jesus" in the Koine Greek has the number 888! The
three-fold 8 probably connotes the tri-une Godhead, "all
the fulness" of which dwells bodily in Jesus (Colossians
2:9). The three-fold 6 in 666 may similarly suggest the
counterfeit trinity of the dragon, the beast, and the false
prophet, all possessing the body of the man of sin.

The full resurrection name of Christ is "Lord Jesus Christ." In the Greek the name "Lord" has a numerical value of 8 × 100 and "Christ" a value of 8 × 185, so the "Lord Jesus Christ" has a numerical value of 8 × 396, which is also the number 176 × 18, where 176 is the number of verses in this 119th Psalm.

Another point of interest is that there are exactly eight combinations of this name ("Lord," "Jesus," "Christ," "Jesus Christ," "Christ Jesus," "Lord Jesus," "Lord Christ," and "Lord Jesus Christ") which are used in the New Testament. In addition to His name, the New Testament uses many titles for Christ. It is perhaps significant that Christ referred to Himself most frequently as the Son of Man, a title which He used just 80 times.

There are, no doubt, many other significant structural and numerical patterns to be found in this tremendous psalm, but these should suffice to make the point that it manifests by its very form that it is divinely inspired. Such designs in the Bible can be explained neither by chance nor by human ingenuity, and thus can only be attributed to God.

Furthermore, there are numerous claims in the psalm itself to the absolute authority and integrity of the Scriptures. For example, note the following:

> I know, O Lord, that thy judgments are right (verse 75).
> Forever, O Lord, thy word is settled in heaven (verse 89).
> I have more understanding than all my teachers; for thy testimonies are my meditation (verse 99).
> I esteem all thy precepts concerning all things to be right (verse 128).
> Thy word is very pure (verse 140).
> The righteousness of thy testimonies is everlasting (verse 144).
> Concerning thy testimonies I have known of old that thou hast founded them forever (verse 152).

Thy word is true from the beginning: and every
one of thy righteous judgments endureth forever
(verse 160).

PURPOSE AND NATURE OF THE PSALM

As noted before, all 176 verses of Psalm 119 stress the
written Word of God. The numerical structure, as well
as its own claims, indicate that it (as well as the entire
Bible) came ultimately from the Spirit of God. However,
the message of the psalm is much more than merely a
testimony to the divine inspiration of the Scriptures.

The Scriptures were inspired for a purpose, "All Scripture is given by inspiration of God . . . that the man of
God may be perfect, throughly furnished unto all good
works" (II Timothy 3:16, 17). This is the primary message of Psalm 119: the holy Scriptures are profitable in
every way and able to meet every need in time and
eternity.

When one first reads this psalm, it seems there is little
or no continuity from one verse to the next. It all seems
like a miscellaneous collection of sayings, arranged in no
particular sequence or order except to fit the acrostic
structure. But it is unlikely that a writer giving such
attention to numeric and alphabetic order would not
give at least as much attention to order of content.

As a matter of fact, the psalm takes on beautiful
significance if one will read it as sort of a spiritual diary,
written at various times during the long life of a believer,
one who has experienced many and varied circumstances of life, but has found the Word of God able
to give guidance and victory in all situations.

The psalm does not itself say that this was the background of its composition, so we cannot be dogmatic.
But since it does not preclude such an interpretation,
and since this does seem to fit so beautifully, we can at
least think of it in this frame of reference. In a way,

therefore, the psalm may record the spiritual growth of
its writer, from his youthful decision to believe and obey
God's Word down to the time when he is expecting
shortly to meet the Lord. Each stanza centers on a
dominant theme, representing the primary experiences
of that stage of his life. At the same time, each stanza
contains "overtones" of other themes, both past and
future, since many experiences in a believer's life are repeated in greater or lesser degree throughout his life.
With this concept in mind, let us journey through his
diary, comparing his circumstances with our own today,
and noting with him that God can meet every need
through His Word.

ALEPH: CONVICTION OF SIN
THROUGH THE WORD
(Verses 1-8)

The first eight verses constitute the writer's recognition that God's blessings are reserved for those who obey
God's laws, followed by an affirmation that he will,
indeed, do just that. But it is significant that only six of
the eight words used in Psalm 119 for the Scriptures
occur in this stanza, and all six emphasize the Scriptures as God's many *commandments.* Thus:

verse 1 — ". . . walk in the law [*torah*] of the Lord."
verse 2 — ". . . keep his testimonies [*eduth*] . . . ."
verse 4 — ". . . keep thy precepts [*piqqudim*] dili-
              gently."
verse 5 — ". . . keep thy statutes! [*chuqqah*]."
verse 6 — ". . . have respect unto all thy *command-
              ments* [*mitzvah*].
verse 7 — ". . . learned thy righteous judgments
              [*mishpat*]."

Resolutions to keep God's commandments are all well
and good, but "by the law is the knowledge of sin"
(Romans 3:20). The better one knows the holiness of
God's statutes, the more he realizes he is unable to

measure up to God's standard. "For as many as are of
the works of the law are under the curse: for it is written,
Cursed is every one that continueth not in all things
which are written in the book of the law to do them"
(Galatians 3:10).

This was the experience of the psalmist. Immediately
after making the sweeping boast "I will keep thy statutes!," he seems to have suddenly been overwhelmed
with the utter impossibility of such a claim and closes
the stanza by throwing himself completely on God's
mercy. "O forsake me not utterly."

BETH: REGENERATION AND
VICTORY BY THE WORD
(Verses 9-16)

In response to his cry and the sincere searching in his
heart (verse 10), God brings cleansing and salvation
through His Word. In this stanza, the last two words for
the Scriptures are used, both of which are translated
"word."

The first verse (9) is powerful. "Wherewithal shall a
young man cleanse his way? by taking heed thereto
according to thy word [dabar]." And then, equally
powerful is verse 11. "Thy word [imrah] have I hid in
mine heart, that I might not sin against thee." The first
"word" speaks of cleansing and the second "word"
speaks of victory over sin. Thus, the Scriptures not only
convict of sin, but also bring regeneration and power to
live a godly life in obedience to God's commandments.
Verse 9 tells of "the washing of water by the word"
(Ephesians 5:26) and verse 11 of being "sanctified"
through the word of truth (John 17:17).

The rest of this stanza stresses the joy of a young
believer, forgiven of sin and desiring to grow in grace
through diligent study of the Scriptures. At the end of
the first stanza he had cried futilely, "I will keep thy

statutes," but at the end of the second stanza, he testifies joyfully, "I will delight myself in thy statutes." The law is no longer a burden, but a delight!

GIMEL: NURTURE AND GROWTH THROUGH THE WORD
(Verses 17-24)

Time and space do not facilitate a verse-by-verse analysis of all the remaining stanzas of Psalm 119, but only an annotation concerning the dominant theme of each stanza, remembering that each stanza also contains overtones from earlier and later themes. Immediately after regeneration, the need is for spiritual growth. "As newborn babes, desire the sincere milk of the word, that ye may grow thereby" (I Peter 2:21). This is the prayer of the young believer in this stanza: "Open thou mine eyes, that I may behold wondrous things out of thy law" (verse 18). "Thy testimonies also are my delight and my counsellors" (verse 24).

DALETH: CONFESSION OF SIN AND RENEWED VICTORY THROUGH THE WORD
(Verses 25-32)

The first flush of joy and victory in a young convert is often followed by a sudden lapse into sin and defeat, from which he must be restored by confessing and forsaking the sin. "My soul cleaveth unto the dust: quicken thou me according to thy word. . . . My soul melteth for heaviness: strengthen thou me according unto thy word. Remove from me the way of lying. . . . I have chosen the way of truth" (verses 25, 28, 29, 30).

HE: CONTINUED INSTRUCTION IN THE
WORD, FOR TRUE
CHARACTER GROWTH
(Verses 33-40)

The godly man does not arrive at spiritual maturity instantaneously. It is a lifelong process, but every stage of that growth must come from the Word. "Teach me, O Lord, the way of thy statutes; and I shall keep it unto the end. . . . Incline my heart unto thy testimonies, and not to covetousness" (verses 33, 36).

VAU: WITNESSING OF THE WORD
TO OTHERS
(Verses 41-48)

The true believer desires to tell of his faith to others and to lead them to salvation, answering their problems and objections through his growing knowledge of God's Word. As Peter commands, we are to "be ready always to give an answer to every man that asketh you, a reason of the hope that is in you" (I Peter 3:15). This was the psalmist's chief concern at this stage of his growth. "So shall I have wherewith to answer him that reproacheth me: for I trust in thy word. . . . I will speak of thy testimonies also before kings, and will not be ashamed" (verses 42, 46).

ZAIN: COMFORT IN SUFFERING,
FROM THE WORD
(Verses 49-56)

As to everyone, a time of suffering came to the writer at this period, probably resulting from his bold testimony. But God's Word was his own answer. "This is my comfort in my affliction: for thy word hath quickened me. . . . Thy statutes have been my songs in the house of my pilgrimage" (verses 50, 54).

CHETH: THE FELLOWSHIP OF BELIEVERS
IN THE WORD
(Verses 57-64)

A pilgrim needs not only the comfort of God and His Word, but also the fellowship of others on the same pilgrimage. "I am a companion of all them that fear thee, and of them that keep thy precepts" (verse 63).

TETH: CHASTISEMENT FOLLOWING
DISOBEDIENCE TO THE WORD
(Verses 65-72)

Suffering is sometimes from God's chastening hand, and this possibility must always be considered at least, even by those who have been faithful in times past. When one continues in disobedience to the teachings of Scripture, God may have to force repentance through chastisement, but this is far better than allowing an erring child to continue uncorrected. "Before I was afflicted I went astray: but now have I kept thy word. . . . It is good for me that I have been afflicted; that I might learn thy statutes" (verses 67, 71).

JOD: SUBMISSION TO GOD'S WORD
UNDER AFFLICTION
(Verses 73-80)

"I know, O Lord, that thy judgments are right, and that thou in faithfulness hast afflicted me. . . . Let my heart be sound in thy statutes: that I be not ashamed" (verses 75, 80).

CEPH: PERSECUTION AND DELIVERANCE, THROUGH THE WORD
(Verses 81-88)

Not all suffering is chastisement, of course, and often the faithful witness will suffer real persecution because of the Word. But the Word is itself the needed comfort and deliverer. "They had almost consumed me upon earth; but I forsook not thy precepts. Quicken me after thy lovingkindness; so shall I keep the testimony of thy mouth" (verses 87, 88).

LAMED: SECURITY IN THE WORD
(Verses 89-96)

The second half of Psalm 119 opens with the tremendous testimony, "Forever, O Lord, thy word is settled in heaven. Thy faithfulness is unto all generations; thou hast established the earth, and it abideth. They continue this day according to thine ordinances; for all are thy servants" (verses 89-91). When one puts his trust in the God of the Bible, he is following no will-o-the-wisp, but the eternal word of the God of creation. That the word is everlasting and immutable is the testimony of many other Scriptures as well (Isaiah 40:8; Matthew 24:35; Psalm 19:9; I Peter 1:24, 25, etc.).

MEM: UNDERSTANDING THE WORD
(Verses 97-104)

The psalmist here returns to the theme of studying the Word, for this is, indeed, a lifelong occupation. "O how love I thy law! It is my meditation all the day . . . . I have more understanding than my teachers: for thy testimonies are my meditation . . . . How sweet are thy words unto my taste! yea, sweeter than honey to my mouth!" (verses 97, 99, 103). As a matter of fact, the older one grows in the Lord and the more varied his experiences and deliverances, the more blessed the Word becomes.

NUN: GUIDANCE BY THE WORD
(Verses 105-112)

Nor does a believer ever grow so mature in spiritual experience as to be able to proceed independently of the Word. "Thy word is a lamp unto my feet, and a light unto my path . . . . Thy testimonies have I taken as an heritage forever: for they are the rejoicing of my heart" (verses 105, 111).

SAMECH: PROTECTION BY GOD'S PROMISES IN THE WORD
(Verses 113-120)

The more powerful the testimony of the believer, the more powerful and bitter become his enemies. But God's Word is adequate for this need, too. "Thou are my hiding place and my shield: I hope in thy word . . . . Thou puttest away all the wicked of the earth like dross: therefore, I love thy testimonies" (verses 114, 119).

AIN: SETTLED OBEDIENCE TO THE WORD
(Verses 121-128)

As the writer continued to grow in grace and knowledge, doubts and rebellions were increasingly vanquished in his mind. "Therefore I love thy commandments above gold; yea, above fine gold. Therefore, I esteem all thy precepts concerning all

things to be right; and I hate every false way"
(verses 127, 128).

PE: LIGHT AND VICTORY
THROUGH THE WORD
(Verses 129-136)

All true instruction must come from the Word of God.
"The entrance of thy words giveth light; it
giveth understanding to the simple" (verse 130).
Through the entering and illuminating Word comes victory in every trial, against both internal and external
dangers. "Order my steps in thy word: and let not any
iniquity have dominion over me. Deliver me from the
oppression of man: so will I keep thy precepts" (verses
133, 134).

TZADDI: ZEAL FOR THE TRUTH
OF GOD'S WORD
(Verses 137-144)

With increasing experience in God's Word comes increasing zeal in its defense because of increasing
confidence in its integrity. "My zeal hath consumed me,
because mine enemies have forgotten thy words. Thy
word is very pure; therefore thy servant loveth
it . . . . The righteousness of thy testimonies is everlasting: give me understanding, and I shall live" (verses 139,
140, 144).

KOPH: INCREASING FAITH
IN THE WORD
(Verses 145-152)

The believer's love and longing for the Word should

continue to increase all his life long. Furthermore, increasing obedience to the Word generates increasing sensitivity to disobedience and a longing to be utterly free from the sin nature which perpetually resists one's growth in the Lord. "I prevented the dawning of the morning, and cried; I hoped in thy word. Mine eyes prevent the night watches, that I might meditate in thy word . . . . Concerning thy testimonies, I have known of old that thou hast founded them forever" (verses 147, 152).

RESH: DELIVERANCE FROM
ALL EVILS BY THE WORD
(Verses 153-160)

"Consider mine affliction and deliver me; for I do not forget thy law. Plead my cause and deliver [same word here as 'redeem'] me: quicken me according to thy word . . . . Thy word is true from the beginning; and every one of thy righteous judgments endureth forever" (verses 153, 154, 160).

SCHIN: SETTLED PEACE
THROUGH THE WORD
(Verses 161-168)

Though oppositions and conflicts with the ungodly continue throughout the believer's life, the Word gives increasing rest and peace. Here the psalmist, who began as a young man, now is old, but enjoying confident peace through his lifelong companionship with the Word of God. "Princes have persecuted me without a cause; but my heart standeth in awe of thy word . . . . Great peace have they which love thy law: and nothing shall offend them . . . . I have kept thy precepts and thy testimonies: for all my ways are before thee" (verses 161, 165, 168).

TAU: FINAL SALVATION
BY THE WORD
(Verses 169-176)

Salvation, of course, is first from the penalty of sin, daily from the power of sin, and ultimately from the presence of sin. As the psalmist neared the end of his long pilgrimage, he increasingly desired to see his Lord. "I have longed for thy salvation, O Lord; and thy law is my delight" (verse 174). Actually the word "salvation" in Hebrew is *yeshua*, the same as "Jesus." The closer one comes to the end of his life and the more conscious he becomes of soon entering into God's presence, the more keenly he becomes aware of his unworthiness, and the more he returns to his first simple faith in the saving grace of God's Word. It is most appropriate, therefore, that Psalm 119 ends as it began, with a simple confession of faith and prayer for salvation; "I have gone astray like a lost sheep; seek thy servant for I do not forget thy commandments."

Chapter 18

GLIMPSES OF CHRIST IN OTHER PSALMS

Several of the Messianic psalms have been examined in this section, all of them pointing to Christ and fulfilled in Him in amazingly accurate detail. In Section II, containing the "scientific" psalms, there were also some specifically Messianic sections (e.g., Psalm 8). Although the scope of this book does not warrant detailed treatment of still other such psalms, there are a number of them which actually do foreshadow Christ in some definite way. Several are directly quoted in the New Testament and said to have been fulfilled in Christ.

The 110th Psalm, for example, is quoted at least ten times with numerous other allusions in the New Testament! "The Lord [i.e., *Jehovah*] said unto my Lord [i.e., *Adonai*], Sit thou on my right hand, until I make thine enemies thy footstool." In this unique first verse of Psalm 110, Jehovah speaks unto Adonai — that is, one person of the Godhead is speaking to another, thus clearly teaching the doctrine of the uni-plurality of the Godhead in the Old Testament as well as the New.

Furthermore, the psalm indicates that "Adonai" has encountered enemies in "Zion" (verse 2) and therefore was caught up to sit at the right hand of "Jehovah" until they would be placed under his feet like a footstool. This prediction clearly presupposes His incarnation, rejection by His people, and His return back to heaven.

Verse 3 further prophesies a "second coming," when His "people shall be willing in the day of thy power." This is amplified in verse 5 by noting that Adonai "shall strike through kings in the day of His wrath."

Also, in verse 4, the remarkable statement is made: "Thou art a priest forever after the order of Melchizedek." This tells us that the divine being Adonai, in His human incarnation, will exercise the ministry of a priest — that is, as an intermediary between God and man — despite the fact that He will not be of the Levitical order of priests, as were all other priests in Israel. *His* priestly ministry, in fact, will continue *forever*! This verse is quoted no less than five times in Hebrews 5, 6, and 7 and is emphatically applied there as fulfilled in the Lord Jesus Christ.

Another very important Messianic chapter is Psalm 118, especially verse 22. "The stone which the builders refused is become the head stone of the corner." This verse is quoted at least four times in the New Testament, stressing that the rejection of Christ by the leaders of the people would only lead ultimately to their own destruction and His exaltation. Jesus said: "And whosoever shall fall on this stone shall be broken: but on whomsoever it shall fall, it will grind him to powder" (Matthew 21:44).

The rejection of Christ at His first coming is also foreseen in a number of the other psalms. For example:

> Yea, mine own familiar friend, in whom I trusted, which did eat of my bread, hath lifted up his heel against me (Psalm 41:9, fulfilled in Christ's betrayal by Judas, as cited in John 13:18, 19).

> I am become a stranger unto my brethren, and an alien unto my mother's children (Psalm 69:8).

> They gave me also gall for my meat, and in my

thirst they gave me vinegar to drink (Psalm 69:
21).

However, His future triumph and reign were also predicted in many of the psalms. The following illustrate
this:

Lift up your heads, O ye gates; and be
ye lift up, ye everlasting doors; and the
King of glory shall come in (Psalm 24:7).

Thou lovest righteousness, and hatest wickedness: therefore God, thy God, hath anointed thee
with the oil of gladness above thy fellows. . . . I
will make thy name to be remembered in all
generations: therefore shall the people praise
thee for ever and ever (Psalm 45:7, 17).

In His days shall the righteous flourish;
and abundance of peace so long as the moon
endureth. He shall have dominion also from sea
to sea, and from the river unto the ends of the
earth (Psalm 72:7, 8).

Also I will make Him my firstborn, higher than
the kings of the earth . . . . Once have I sworn by
my holiness that I will not lie unto David. His
seed shall endure for ever, and His throne as the
sun before me (Psalm 89:27, 35-36).

The departure of Christ into the world from heaven at
the time of His incarnation is beautifully pictured in
Psalm 45:8:

All thy garments smell of myrrh, and aloes,
and cassia, out of the ivory palaces, whereby they
have made thee glad.

Conversely, His ascension back into heaven is portrayed
in Psalm 68:18 and is quoted with this application in
Ephesians 4:8.

Thou hast ascended on high, thou hast led
captivity captive; thou hast received
gifts for men; yea, for the rebellious also,
that the Lord God might dwell among them.

The perfections of His character and the righteousness

of his acts are noted in many of the psalms. The following are typical:

Who shall ascend into the hill of the Lord? or who shall stand in His holy place? He that hath clean hands, and a pure heart; who hath not lifted up His soul unto vanity, nor sworn deceitfully (Psalm 24:3, 4).

Thou art fairer than the children of men: grace is poured into thy lips: therefore God hath blessed thee for ever (Psalm 45:2).

He shall judge the people with righteousness, and thy poor with judgment (Psalm 72:2).

Some of these Messianic psalms (notably Psalms 24, 45, 72, 89, 110, 118, and others) are well deserving of detailed, verse-by-verse study in order to get the full impact of their testimony of Christ.

The point has surely been made by now. In the book of Psalms, the many marvelous prophetic foregleams of the Lord Jesus Christ testify with great power both to His own majestic deity and to the amazing divine inspiration of the Scriptures.

PART FOUR

THE PILGRIM PSALMS AND THE CHRISTIAN LIFE

Chapter 19

THE SONGS OF DEGREES

Immediately after Psalm 119, the longest chapter in the Bible, is found a series of fifteen remarkable short psalms known as the Songs of Degrees. Each one has that phrase in its traditional title, but there has been much difference of opinion among Bible scholars as to its exact significance. The middle one (Psalm 127) is entitled "A Song of Degrees for Solomon;" two in the first half (122 and 124) and two in the second half (131 and 133) are each entitled " A Song of Degrees of David." The remaining ten (five in the first half and five in the second half) are entirely anonymous, each being called simply a "A Song of Degrees."

The word translated "degrees" is the Hebrew *maalah,* often translated "steps," "stairs," etc. It means literally "going up to a higher place." Most authorities believe these psalms were sung by the children of Israel as they traveled from their homes to Jerusalem for the annual ascent up to the higher elevations on which the holy city was built.

The themes do seem appropriate for such a use,

proceeding as they do from the great cry of spiritual need
in Psalm 120 up to the joyful note of blessing and unity
on Zion and in the temple, the themes of Psalms 133 and
134. There is an obvious spiritual parallel in the journey
of a believer through life, from the time of the conviction
of sin and his cry for salvation until his final exaltation
in glory. The psalms may thus well be regarded as
depicting fifteen stages in a spiritual "pilgrim's
progress." This concept is somewhat similar to the concept of the 22 chapters in the believer's diary as
suggested in our exposition of Psalm 119, which immediately precedes these Songs of Degrees.

POSSIBLE BACKGROUND
AND AUTHORSHIP

Even assuming that these psalms were indeed sung by
pilgrims on the way to Jerusalem, that does not mean
they were originally composed or compiled for this purpose. Except for the four psalms attributed to David and
one possibly authored by Solomon, no one really knows
why, when, or by whom they were written.

One very plausible suggestion, however, supported by
certain circumstantial evidences, is that they should be
attributed to the great king Hezekiah, commemorating
his recovery from a fatal sickness and the deliverance of
Judah and Jerusalem from the armies of the Assyrians.
The story of the deliverance and healing was apparently
originally reported by the prophet Isaiah (Isaiah 36-38),
and it was later incorporated almost verbatim into the
historical books (II Kings 18-20), a remarkable fact
which perhaps indicated the importance attributed to
the event by the Jewish scribes who later brought
together the two Books of Kings.

It will be recalled that Sennacherib's hosts had in-
vaded Judah and laid siege to Jerusalem. The leader of
the host, Rabshakeh, had made a series of blasphemous
threats against Hezekiah and the Jews, and Hezekiah
had desperately prayed to God for deliverance. God had

heard his prayer and saved Jerusalem by a mighty miracle.

Soon after that, Hezekiah experienced another miracle. He was about to die, but again prayed to the Lord for deliverance, and God answered, through Isaiah, once again:

> Then came the word of the Lord to Isaiah, saying, Go, and say to Hezekiah, Thus saith the Lord, the God of David thy father, I have heard thy prayer, I have seen thy tears: behold, I will add unto thy days fifteen years. And I will deliver thee and this city out of the hand of the king of Assyria: and I will defend this city. And this shall be a sign unto thee from the Lord, that the Lord will do this thing that He hath spoken; Behold, I will bring again the shadow of the degrees, which is gone down by the sundial of Ahaz, ten degrees backward. So the sun returned ten degrees, by which degrees it was gone down (Isaiah 38:4-8).

The "degrees" by which the sun's shadow returned on the dial is the same word as is used in "Songs of Degrees." The "10 degrees" were the sign that Hezekiah's life would be miraculously extended by "15 years." The suggestion has been made, therefore, that Hezekiah composed ten psalms, one for each degree, and that he added four more unpublished psalms of David's plus the one "for Solomon," possibly also written by David, to make a total of 15, one for each year of his prolonged life.

Immediately after the miracle, in fact, Hezekiah had composed one psalm of thanksgiving (Isaiah 38:9-20), which ended with this promise: "The living, the living, he shall praise thee, as I do this day: the father to the children shall make known the truth. The Lord was ready to save me: therefore we will sing my songs to the stringed instruments all the days of our life in the house of the Lord" (Isaiah 38:19-20).

These "songs to the stringed instruments" (one word in the Hebrew, *neginoth*) may thus have been these fifteen songs of degrees, just as "all the days of our life" were his fifteen years. An additional reason why Hezekiah and his descendants, "the father to the children" regarded this miracle as so important is the fact that he actually had no children at the time! God's great promise to David (II Samuel 7:13) would have failed had Hezekiah died at this time, since his first son was not born until three years after his healing (II Kings 21:1).

THEME OF THE SONGS

The most obvious theme of the fifteen psalms is what has been called "the hope of Israel," the great plan and promises associated with Israel and Jerusalem in the economy of God. This theme dominates most of the psalms and is assumed in the others (note, for example, 121:4; 122:1-6; 125:1-2; 126:1; 128:5-6; 129:5; 130:7-8; 131:3; 132:13; 133:3; 134:3; etc.)

Certain numerical features may also be noted: The word "Israel" occurs 7 times in these songs, the word "Zion" occurs 7 times, and the words "Jacob" and "Jerusalem" together occur a total of 7 times.

Although God's relation to Israel is the primary theme of these psalms, we have already noted that a broader theme may well be that of the spiritual pilgrimage of a believer through life. The theme of deliverance from enemies, as experienced by Hezekiah, also recurs frequently, giving support to the idea of his original authorship, as does the frequent mention of God's promise of the seed to David and the blessing of children in general.

Chapter 20
THE CRY FOR SALVATION
(Psalm 120)

The songs of the degrees begin with a cry of distress to the Lord, calling for deliverance from "lying lips" and the deceitful and false tongue, lips that hate peace and desire war. One can almost hear the insolent harangue of Rabshakeh and Hezekiah's desperate plea to God for deliverance.

The reference in verse 5 to dwelling in Mesech and Kedar is rather cryptic, since Mesech was in the far north and Kedar probably south in the Arabian desert. Mesech (same as Meshech) was originally one of Noah's grandsons, whose descendants traveled north from Babel and eventually into what is now Russia, their name still reflected in the names Moscow and Muscovite. Kedar was a son of Ishmael (Genesis 25:13) and one of the ancestors of the Arabs. There is perhaps a prophetic note here, since both the Russians and Arabs were to be particular enemies of Israel in the latter days.

More likely, the lament is a figure of speech for living far from home in an enemy land. Spiritually, it would answer to one of God's elect under conviction of sin but still living in the ungodly world ruled by the great adversary, the father of all lying lips and deceitful tongues. "My soul hath long dwelt with him that hateth peace" (verse 5). The only answer to the need of an unsaved soul is the Lord, and finally he seeks and finds the God of peace. "In my distress I cried unto the Lord, and He heard me. Deliver my soul, O Lord" (verse 1, 2). Something like this experience has been shared by every redeemed soul; the Lord always hears and delivers all who call on Him in repentance and faith.

Chapter 21

THE ASSURANCE
OF SALVATION
(Psalm 121)

The first verse of Psalm 121 is often misquoted because of a poor choice of punctuation (the original Hebrew was not punctuated but was interpreted according to context). A proper reading would be as follows: "Shall I lift up mine eyes unto the hills? From whence cometh my help?" Then the question is answered. "My help cometh from the Lord, which made heaven and earth."

There is nothing in the hills that could provide help to a needy soul, as the usual punctuation might suggest. As a matter of fact, the prophets were frequently called on by God to condemn and destroy the "high places," where the people were continually being tempted to lapse into idolatry and worship the host of heaven. God had commanded through Moses: "Ye shall utterly destroy all the places, wherein the nations which ye shall possess served their gods, upon the high mountains, and upon the hills, and under every green tree" (Deuteronomy 12:2).

There is a perverseness in man which makes him

desire to "worship and serve the creation more than the Creator" (Romans 1:25), to be nature-worshippers, and worshippers of the personified forces of nature. The entire system of paganism, and its modern counterpart, evolutionism, is based on such worship. But nature in itself is without power to save. No wonder Jeremiah cried: "Truly in vain is salvation hoped for from the hills, and from the multitude of mountains: truly in the Lord our God is the salvation of Israel" (Jeremiah 3:23).

The psalmist was not looking to the hills for help! He was calling on the one who had made heaven and earth. The seeking sinner of the first Song of Degrees thus becomes the secure believer of the second Song. The lesson in type is most appropriate today, for the worship of nature in one form or another abounds as never before in history. True salvation can only be found by calling on the great Creator of the universe. He alone is able to save, but He is indeed able to save to the uttermost all who call upon Him (Hebrews 7:25).

And that Creator, of course, is none other than Jesus Christ! He made everything in heaven and earth as God (Colossians 1:16) and has been given all power in heaven and earth as man (Matthew 28:18).

Then follows one of the most remarkable testimonies of assurance and security for the believer to be found anywhere in Scripture. The word "keep" (also translated "keeper" and "preserve") occurs no less than six times in five verses (3, 4, 5, 7, 8). "The Lord is thy keeper." Whether day or night is immaterial, because "He that keepeth thee" will neither slumber nor sleep. Whether attacked by evil men or evil circumstances does not matter because "the Lord shall preserve thee from *all* evil." Though the whole world may lie in the wicked one, yet "He that is begotten of God keepeth him, and that wicked one toucheth him not" (I John 5:18, 19). Furthermore, "He shall preserve thy soul." The Father will answer the Son's prayer: "Holy Father, keep through thine own name those whom thou hast given me" (John 17:11). "The Lord is thy defense [same word as 'shade'] upon thy right hand." "Neither shall any one pluck them out of my hand!" (John 10:29).

Then in a final all-comprehensive promise, He assures the believer He will preserve him in every circumstance of this life, whether "going out or coming in," and then in heaven "even for evermore." The soul that cried to the Lord for help has put his trust in the great Creator, who also is the Savior, and has thus found a secure salvation and everlasting life.

Chapter 22

FELLOWSHIP IN THE HOUSE OF GOD
(Psalm 122)

Immediately after receiving salvation and the assurance of salvation, the most important step for a new believer to take next is to unite with the Lord's people in the institution established for that very purpose, a local church. It is appropriate that the next "degree" is Psalm 122, which has the theme of fellowship in God's house. "I was glad when they said unto me, Let us go into the house of the Lord" (verse 1).

Just as "Hezekiah went up into the house of the Lord, and spread it before the Lord" (Isaiah 38:14), when he prayed for Jerusalem's deliverance, and just as "the tribes go up, the tribes of the Lord, unto the testimony of Israel, to give thanks unto the name of the Lord" (Psalm 122:4), so believers today should go to "the house of God, which is the church of the living God, the pillar and ground of the truth" (I Timothy 3:15). The widespread practice of believers today of neglecting their "local church, established by Christ for the fellowship and growth of His followers, in favor of various interdenominational organizations and of commuting from one church to another, is unfortunate and unscriptural.

The theme of the national hope of Israel itself is dominant in this psalm, however. Not only the ancient pilgrims but also the future regathered and redeemed Israelites will "stand within thy gates, O Jerusalem," where will be "set thrones of judgment, the thrones of the house of David" (verses 2, 5, also Isaiah 9:6, 7; Ezekiel 34:23, 24; 37:21-25; Luke 1:32; 22:29, 30). "Pray for the peace of Jerusalem" (verse 6). Jerusalem ("the city of peace") has seldom known real peace throughout its long history, but in that coming day, this prayer will be answered. "For out of Zion shall go forth the law, and the word of the Lord from Jerusalem. And He shall judge among the nations, and shall rebuke many people: . . . nation shall not lift up sword against nation, neither shall they learn war any more" (Isaiah 2:3, 4).

Though the primary reference is to Jerusalem and its temple, it is certainly appropriate in this present age to heed its spiritual lesson relative to the heavenly Jerusalem in its present local manifestation, namely, the church of the Lord Jesus. "For my brethren and companions' sakes, I will now say, Peace be within thee. Because of the house of the Lord our God I will seek thy good" (verses 8, 9).

Chapter 23

FERVENT PRAYER FOR URGENT NEEDS
(Psalm 123)

The 123rd Psalm contains only four verses, but its theme is all-important. The sinner must call upon God for salvation (Psalm 121), but the believer must then continue to call upon God for deliverance from every enemy and for the supply of every need. Though he has been delivered from this present evil world (Galatians 1:4) as far as his eternal destiny is concerned, he is still very much in the world physically.

Just as for his salvation, his daily help must come from the God of creation. "Unto thee lift I up mine eyes, O thou that dwellest in the heavens" (verse 1). There is no more a question of whether he should lift up his eyes to the hills (Psalm 121:1), for he knows there is no help from any source but the God of heaven. The believer should very early acquire the practice of daily seeking the will and the mercy of the Lord, "looking unto Jesus" only (Hebrews 12:2). He is our master, we are His servants. Therefore, "our eyes wait upon the Lord our God." Three times the psalmist cries for God's mercy. We must never think we *deserve* God's favor; it is always by His grace.

The godly man, truly trusting in God alone, will always be the object of contempt and scorning from those who are proud of their own accomplishments and at ease in the present world. It was true with godly King Hezekiah, enduring the blasphemous scorn of Rabshakeh and Sennacharib. But God delivered him in answer to believing prayer and will do the same for His people in any age.

Chapter 24

ANSWERED PRAYER FROM THE GOD OF CREATION
(Psalm 124)

Psalm 123 records the desperate prayer of a believer in danger from the ungodly; Psalm 124 is his testimony of answered prayer. The one follows the other as sure as day follows night, because the Lord is on *our* side, not *their* side!

The "little flock" of God (Luke 12:32) has "but little strength" (Revelation 3:8) of its own, compared to the tremendous resources of the world's political and educational establishments. But these overwhelming odds merely give God a chance to "show Himself strong in the behalf of them whose heart is perfect toward Him" (II Chronicles 16:9).

But we must never make the mistake of relying on some other defense or some other power, because these will inevitably fail. They themselves are part of the world system and so cannot long prevail in a fight against it! "If it had not been the Lord who was on our side, when men rose up against us; Then they had swallowed us up quick, when their wrath was kindled against us" (verses 2, 3). The proud waters would have overwhelmed our souls, but "when the enemy shall come in like a flood, the Spirit of the Lord shall lift up a standard against him" (Isaiah 59:19). We are like birds ensnared in a trap devised by the deceivers in the world system, but the Lord will not allow His own to become a prey to such as these. He will, in good time, make a way of escape and the snare is broken. Even as the psalmist had recognized when he first sought salvation, he returns again to the same Savior for every deliverance, to the God who created all things and who therefore controls all things. "Our help is in the name of the Lord, who made heaven and earth" (Psalm 121:1; 124:8).

Chapter 25

GROWTH IN FAITH AND REST IN GOD
(Psalm 125)

As one grows older in the Lord, experiencing time after time His mercies and answers to prayer, he becomes stronger in faith, no longer fearful when trials and adversities abound. Having seen God often turn defeat into victory and darkness into light, the believer is increasingly confident that "the Lord is round about His people from henceforth even for ever" (Psalm 125:2). "And we know that all things work together for good to them that love God" (Romans 8:28).

The 125th Psalm thus speaks of settled trust in God, with perfect peace for those whose minds are stayed on Him (Isaiah 26:3). "They that trust in the Lord shall be as mount Zion, which cannot be removed, but abideth for ever" (verse 1), and "peace shall be upon Israel" (verse 5).

There is also recognition that, though the wicked may sometimes appear to prosper in this world, eventually "the Lord shall lead them forth" into judgment. Furthermore, "the rod of the wicked shall not rest upon the lot of the righteous." That is, the wicked shall not be able to govern the actions of the righteous. His "sceptre" shall not rule over that possession which has been given to the righteous. No matter how strong the pressure, God "will make a way to escape, that ye may be able to bear it" (I Corinthians 10:13). Indeed, the Lord *will* "do good unto those that be good, and to them that are upright in their hearts" (verse 4).

Chapter 26

TEARFUL SOWING AND JOYFUL REAPING
(Psalm 126)

The first verse of this beautiful psalm refers to the "captivity of Zion" and thus offers one of the main reasons why many commentators believe the "Songs of Degrees" were written after the return from the Babylonian captivity. As already noted, however, four of them are attributed to David and one to Solomon, and there is much internal evidence that they were written or gathered originally by King Hezekiah. Even Psalm 126 easily yields to that interpretation, with the "captivity" a very apt term for the long siege of Sennacherib. The sudden miraculous deliverance from that captivity would indeed have generated exactly such joyful laughter and singing in the city of Zion as the psalm describes. Note how naturally the words fit this great occasion:

When the Lord turned again [literally "converted"] the captivity of Zion, we were like them that dream. Then was our mouth filled with laughter, and our tongue with singing: then said

they among the heathen, The Lord hath done
great things for them.

This was indeed the reaction of the heathen, according
to II Chronicles 32:23. "And many brought gifts unto the
Lord to Jerusalem, and presents to Hezekiah King of
Judah: so that He was magnified in the sight of all nations from thenceforth."

In the spiritual analogue, of course, this "conversion"
from captivity must refer to the miracle of salvation and
regeneration. How often have these words been appropriated by believers to their own experiences. "The
Lord *hath* done great things for us; whereof we are
glad!" The new surge of living water through a believer's
life (John 7:38) when he is set free from his bondage to
the old life of sin and death is like the dry watercourses
in the southern wilderness (the "south," the *Negev*) suddenly bursting with streams of water after long-awaited
rains.

Hezekiah had "wept sore" before the Lord (Isaiah
38:3) when praying for healing from his fatal sickness.
When the Lord heard and healed him, having "seen his
tears" (Isaiah 38:5), Hezekiah composed his psalm of
thanksgiving, and vowed to sing before the Lord all the
days of his life. He had sown in tears, but reaped in joy,
and this was the result of a special experience subsequent to his even greater experience of victory over
Sennacherib.

The psalmist compares such experiences to the difficult labor of seed-sowing. Because of sin, the ground is
cursed, and man must eat his bread in the sweat of his
face (Genesis 3:17) and in sorrow, all the days of his life.
To accomplish the work of maintaining physical life and
the even more difficult work of bringing spiritual life to
those dead in sins, blood and sweat and tears are often
required. Even the Lord Jesus, like Hezekiah, "in the
days of His flesh, . . . offered up prayers and supplications with strong crying and tears unto Him that was
able to save Him from death . . ." (Hebrews 5:7).

Hezekiah needed to live in order to have the son God

had promised, and God saw his earnest tears and
answered his prayer. The sowing of seed was applied in
the New Testament by the Lord Jesus to the work of
spreading the Word of God (Luke 8:11), in His great
parable of the sower. Psalm 126 thus in retrospect
becomes a beautiful picture and promise of fruitful witnessing. "He that goeth forth and weepeth, bearing
precious seed, shall doubtless come again with rejoicing,
bringing his sheaves with him."

No seed is so precious as the Word (Psalm
19:10; 119:72) and no joy so great as that of bringing
forth spiritual life as fruit from sowing the Word. This is
an important part of the life of a believer, both sowing
and reaping. The sowing must be both individually
compassionate, as was that of Christ (Mark 6:34) and
yet also cast abroad as widely as possible, for all need it.
"Cast thy bread upon the waters: for thou shalt find it
after many days. . . . He that observeth the wind shall
not sow; and he that regardeth the clouds shall not
reap. . . . In the morning sow thy seed, and in the eve-
ning withhold not thine hand: for thou knowest not
whether shall prosper, either this or that, or whether
they both shall be alike good" (Ecclesiastes 11:1, 4, 6).

There are tears involved in the sowing, but the
promise of joy in the reaping. "And he that reapeth
receiveth wages, and gathereth fruit unto life eternal:
that both he that soweth and he that reapeth may rejoice together" (John 4:36).

Chapter 27

CHILDREN IN THE LORD
(Psalm 127)

Psalm 126 contains the promise of a fruitful harvest following industrious and difficult sowing. Psalm 127 is actual testimony of the harvest and its blessings, no longer described figuratively as a field of grain, but as a fruitful home, with an abundance of children.

These children may well be either actual physical progeny or spiritual children in the Lord. God's first command to mankind was to "be fruitful and multiply" (Genesis 1:28). This command was repeated after the Flood (Genesis 9:1) and has never been withdrawn, even in the prophetic context of a latter-day supposed population explosion. Godly parents especially should pray and work to have large families, so that they can "bring them up in the nurture and admonition of the Lord" (Ephesians 6:4), thereby multiplying not only their descendants but also their ministry and witness.

The Scriptures often teach that children in a home constitute a sign of God's favor (e.g., Deuteronomy 28:1-4), though, of course, this is not necessarily a universal principle. This 127th Psalm occupies the central position in the Songs of Degrees, and the middle verse of this central psalm is the strongest testimony to this effect to be found in the Bible. "Lo, children are an heritage of the Lord: and the fruit of the womb is His reward" (verse 3). Then the next verse, which is actually the middle verse of the entire 15-psalm assemblage, emphasizes this truth by another figure: "As arrows are in the hand of a mighty man; so are children of the youth."

One can almost see Hezekiah wistfully penning these words, perhaps copying from an old psalm written for Solomon (who, with his thousand wives and concubines probably had as many children as any man in history) and hoping that God would be willing to give him at least one son in his old age! As we have noted, his son and successor, Manasseh, was not born until three years after his miraculous healing (II Kings 20:6; 21:1).

"Happy is the man that hath his quiver full of them." Continuing with the figure of children as weapons, it is stressed that *many* children — enough to fill the "quiver" — are good. Especially those who were children of the youth will be grown and vigorous men when their father is growing too old for effective combat in the battle against the enemy in the gate, whether that enemy is an actual physical combatant or the great Enemy of the souls of men.

It should always be remembered however, that such blessings in the home and in the nation do not come automatically just because there are many children or many citizens. "Except the Lord build the house, they labour in vain that build it; except the Lord keep the city, the watchman waketh but in vain" (verse 1). No amount of effort or scheming or fretting will accomplish the work — whether that work be a home, a church, a college, a city, or a nation. If it is the Lord's work then it's the *Lord's* work, and He will see it through according to His own good will.

Though the curse is still on the earth, and it is man's province to eat his bread in sorrow (Genesis 3:17), Christ has redeemed us from the curse of the Law (Galatians

3:13). He giveth His beloved sleep instead of fear, rest instead of labor, joy in place of sorrow.

All of these wonderful blessings apply to physical children, and yet much more to spiritual children, fruit not of the womb but of the Word. Whether or not God chooses to bless one of His children with a mate and family, every believer has the privilege of sowing the good seed, and thus producing spiritual children. Happy, indeed, is the Christian whose quiver is full of them.

Chapter 28

FRUITFULNESS AND GODLY MATURITY
(Psalm 128)

Psalm 128 continues the theme of Psalm 127, speaking of the blessings of a house built by the Lord, with a God-fearing father walking in the will of the Lord (verse 1). Such a man, God promises (in both verse 1 and verse 4), will be blessed with a fruitful wife and sturdy children, strong and durable as the olive plant (verse 3).

Not only would there be many children born (the theme of Psalm 127), but these children would be a joy in the home, especially in the blessed times of fellowship around the family table, and they in turn would then beget children of their own, bringing still more blessing to the family circle.

There need be no concern that such a large family would be too expensive to feed, for "thou shalt eat the labour of thine hands; happy shalt thou be; and it shall be well with thee" (verse 2).

These are wonderful promises and many, many godly families can testify to its literal fulfillment in their own experiences. On the other hand, there have undoubtedly been many families of equal spirituality who have, in one way or another, failed as yet to experience their *literal* fulfilment. That is, some men of great godliness (e.g., the Apostle Paul) never even acquired a wife at all. There were no doubt some godly families carried into captivity from Jerusalem during the time of Nebuchadnezzar and who, therefore, did not really "see the good of Jerusalem all the days of thy life" (verse 5). Many similar families have experienced sickness, tragedy, and heartbreak in their children, and some have, through no fault of their own, been childless.

Thus, the main thrust of these promises (though often fulfilled literally as evidence of God's genuine concern for His divine institution of the human family) must be in its spiritual principles. *Every* man who truly fears the Lord and walks in his ways will see the birth and growth of many spiritual children. (Even if not in this life, he will see them in the *new* "Jerusalem all the days of thy [eternal] life.") Just as literal children are begotten from a fruitful wife, so are spiritual sons begotten with the Word of truth (James 1:18) from the fruitful ground of honest and good hearts (Luke 8:15). It is, in fact, God who gives the increase. "The Lord shall bless thee out of Zion" (verse 5), and such a man will even have the joy of seeing his spiritual grandchildren to many generations, after the Lord's return, when there will be everlasting "peace upon Israel" (verse 6).

Chapter 29

LIFELONG PRESERVATION AMIDST OPPOSITION
(Psalm 129)

As the mature believer continues to witness for the Lord through the years, he will encounter opposition and persecution, sometimes open and violent, more commonly covert and insidious. Looking back over the years, he can testify: "Many a time have they afflicted me from my youth, yet they have not prevailed against me" (verses 1, 2). Sometimes he had been, as it were, cut deeply, like a plow furrowing the ground, or restrained, as one bound with cords, but the Lord always eventually healed the wounds and broke the chains.

Not only is the righteous man protected but, eventually the wicked man is judged, because "the Lord is righteous" (verse 4). The great host of those who "hate Zion" have, one by one, been "confounded and turned back" (verse 5). In contrast to the true believer, whose roots are deep and whose branches are fruitful (as in Psalms 127 and 128), the wicked are like grass attempting to grow on a housetop. Where there can be no roots (Colossians 2:7) there will be no harvest. The one who sows good seed on good ground will bring many sheaves (Psalm 127:6).

Though such haters of Zion may for a while be much esteemed by the world, eventually all will recognize them for what they are, and those who "go by," observing their eternal barrenness, will see that God's blessing is not on them, and so will not *ask* God's blessing on them (verse 8). "And they shall go forth, and look upon the carcases of the men that have transgressed against me: for their worm shall not die, neither shall their fire be quenched; and they shall be an abhorring unto all flesh" (Isaiah 66:24).

Chapter 30

LONGING FOR THE LORD'S COMING
(Psalm 130)

The subject seems suddenly to change in the 130th Psalm. Instead of primary attention directed to his family or to his opponents, the believer now is thinking only of his own relation to the Lord and of his desire to be with Him. He has been through deep waters, perhaps fallen into some sin of which he is deeply ashamed. The sense of the Lord's blessing and fellowship, which had been his portion for so long, had been withdrawn, and he was under great conviction.

Every Christian has been through such an experience, and the waters can, indeed, be very deep, until repentance and confession lead to the Lord's return in blessing once again. "If we say that we have no sin, we deceive ourselves, and the truth is not in us. If we confess our sins, He is faithful and just to forgive us our sins, and to cleanse us from all unrighteousness" (I John 1:8, 9).

A real believer, of course, will be chastened of the Lord when he sins (Hebrews 12:5-11), and he does well to take the course described here by the psalmist: "Out of the depths have I cried unto thee, O Lord [*Jehovah*], Lord [*Adonai*], hear my voice; let thine ears be attentive to the voice of my supplications. If thou, Lord [*Jehovah*], shouldest mark iniquities, O Lord, [*Adonai*] who shall stand? But there is forgiveness with thee, that thou mayest be feared" (verses 1-4).

The alternating use of the two divine names (*Jehovah* and *Adonai*) is striking. The same sequence occurs in verses 5 and 6 again. It is as though the psalmist were, in his anxious search for cleansing, invoking every attribute of the divine Name. He does, indeed, find forgiveness, as did David (Psalms 32, 51, 143) and as all do even today who come to the Lord Jesus in sincere confession and trust.

Verses 5 and 6 are two of the most beautiful expressions of faith in the Lord's coming to be found in Scripture. "I wait for the Lord, my soul doth wait, and in His word do I hope. My soul waiteth for the Lord more than they that watch for the morning." The primary thought, of course, is that of longing for the light of God's presence and the joy of His salvation after the dark night of conviction and chastisement experienced because of sin in his life as a believer. The expression "wait for" could as well be rendered "expect." One has the right to *expect* forgiveness and cleansing from the Lord when he has met the condition of repentance and confession, because this is God's promise. "In His *word* do I hope!" It is significant that this is one of only two explicit references to the word of God in all the fifteen psalms of degrees, in striking contrast to the 176 references to it in the great psalm which immediately precedes them (the other is in Psalm 132:12).

The repetition of the phrase "they that watch for the morning" (verse 6) indicates particular significance to the concept of watching for the Lord. This is an important admonition, apparently, just as it was important for the temple night watchman to watch intently for the first sign of dawn in the eastern sky, as he called out the hours through the night (comp. Isaiah 21:11, 12).

Though the primary reference is to waiting for the Lord's forgiveness and restoration, this is only a type of the complete deliverance of the believer from the very presence of sin when the Lord returns to bring salvation to all the earth. The stress on watching for the Lord in this psalm certainly justifies our making this secondary application, especially in light of the frequent New Testament exhortations to watch for His coming (e.g., Hebrews 9:28; II Timothy 4:8; Matthew 24:42; Luke 21:36). "Watch ye therefore: for ye know not when the master of the house cometh, at even, or at midnight, or at the cockcrowing, or in the morning; Lest coming suddenly He find you sleeping. And what I say unto you, I say unto all, Watch" (Mark 13:35-37).

In the spiritual analogue which we have been following in these Songs of Degrees, it is appropriate that this great theme (both of increased dependence on the Lord's forgiving mercy and of watching for His imminent coming) should be introduced toward the end of the believer's stay on earth. The older one grows in the Lord, the more conscious he becomes of his own unworthiness and the more anxious he becomes to see His Savior. "For with the Lord there is mercy, and with Him is plenteous redemption" (verse 7). Finally, at His second coming, there will be full blessing for the redeemed of the chosen people. "And so all Israel shall be saved: as it is written, There shall come out of Sion the Deliverer, and shall turn away ungodliness from Jacob" (Romans 11:26). "And He shall redeem Israel from all his iniquities" (verse 8).

Chapter 31

COMPLETE HOPE
IN THE LORD
(Psalm 131)

This brief psalm, only three verses long, speaks particularly of the believer's settled conviction of God's sovereignty in all things and his complete confidence in God's goodness. Such an assurance represents the testimony of long experience in the Lord and long delight in His Word.

"Lord, my heart is not haughty nor mine eyes lofty." There is no longer room for personal pride, when one finally becomes persuaded that only God is lofty. "Neither do I exercise myself in great matters, or in things too high for me" (verse 1). How many and how endless — how inconclusive — have been the controversies over predestination and free will, over divine sovereignty and human responsibility. The Scriptures teach that both are true, but men try to argue one or the other, arrogantly believing they can rationalize one in terms of the other, or the other in terms of the one. But such infinite comprehension is possible only for the infinite God, and the heart confirms what the Scriptures teach, that man is free and responsible while God is simultaneously sovereign and all-predestinating. Our finite minds cannot resolve such an infinite paradox, but we don't have to do so. Such "things are too high for me." "Such knowledge is too wonderful for me; it is high, I cannot attain unto it" (Psalm 139:6).

The counsels of God need not be explained to the believer, because he knows that whatever God does is good, by definition. He simply trusts. "I have quieted myself as a child" (verse 2). Like a weaned child, he is mature enough to make his choices, but innocent enough to trust his parents.

God's promises are unchangeable and His power to implement them irresistible. Therefore we may "hope in the Lord from henceforth and for ever" (verse 3). Happy is the mature believer in Christ who has come to such a settled faith.

Chapter 32

PRAYING FOR
THE KINGDOM
(Psalm 132)

Not only does the strong Christian desire to see the Lord, but he also desires to see the accomplishment of God's purposes on earth. It is one thing to desire the Lord's return in order to be delivered from our troubles; it is another to desire to see His will done on earth as it is in heaven, simply because we love Him and His will! It is indication of yet greater maturity of faith and love when we come to desire the fulfillment of His promises and His great purposes on the earth, not for our own comfort and joy, but for *His* glory!

This is the underlying theme of Psalm 132, which is the longest of the Songs of Degrees. The writer is especially concerned with the promises God had made to David concerning the coming Messianic kingdom. If Hezekiah was the author or compiler of these Songs, as we have inferred, it reflects his own concern lest he die before he had a son who would be able to continue the line of descent specified in the promises. In answer to Hezekiah's prayer, God had assured him: "For I will defend this city to save it, for mine own sake, and for my

servant David's sake" (II Kings 19:34; 20:6). This
language is very similar to that of the prayer in Psalm
132:10: "For thy servant David's sake turn not away the
face of thine anointed." It is of course, especially significant that the word "anointed" (Hebrew *Messiah* =
Christ) is used here and also in verse 17: "There will I
make the horn of David to bud: I have ordained a lamp
for mine anointed [i.e., 'Christ']."

The psalmist rehearses the background of God's
promise to David, urging God to remember David's
desire to build God a house and God's responding promise to build David's house. It might seem almost
presumptuous for a believer to "remind" God of His
promises, but as a matter of fact God seems to delight in
this. There are many such prayers recorded in the
psalms (e.g. Psalm 119:49) and in the prophets (e.g.,
Jeremiah 14:21). Hezekiah himself had called on God to
remember (Isaiah 38:3). It almost seems as though God
frequently waits until his people are earnest enough to
study His word and to call upon Him to fulfill His word,
before He acts on it.

The exact breakdown of Psalm 132 into its component
parts is difficult, with much difference of opinion among
commentators. The following appears the most plausible outline in the context of the inferred Hezekian origin
of the Songs of Degrees.

Verses 1-2.	Prayer of Hezekiah
Verses 3-5.	Prayer of David as quoted by Hezekiah
Verses 6-10.	Continued prayer of Hezekiah
Verses 11-18.	Response of God to David, as confirmed to Hezekiah.

Twice (verses 2, 5), God is called "the Mighty One of
Jacob." This is a very unusual name for God, occurring
elsewhere only in Isaiah 49:26 and Isaiah 60:16 (Isaiah,
of course, being a contemporary of Hezekiah) and in
Genesis 49:24 (from which it no doubt was derived),
where it was first used in connection with Jacob's dying

blessing on his sons. The psalmist, in using such a name, stressed that God's promises applied not only to Judah but to all Israel, and that His might was ample to accomplish them.

Verse 6 is particularly difficult: "Lo, we heard of it at Ephratah: We found it in the fields of the wood." Ephratah is the ancient name of Bethlehem (where God's "anointed" one was born, a term applying both to David and to Christ) and, by Hebrew parallelism, the "fields of the wood" is probably either synonymous or directly related. Many have identified it with Kirjath-jearim, where the ark was kept for a while, but this identification seems nebulous (even though *jearim* means "woods"). Since the psalm is both prophetic and messianic, it may well be a prophecy of the coming of the Anointed One to His people. The people of Israel first "heard" of His birth while in the fields near Bethlehem (Luke 2:8, 15, 16), and they "found" His "habitation," not in the mighty temple but in a lowly manger. One can almost hear the Judaean shepherds saying: "We will go into his tabernacles: we will worship at His footstool" (verse 7).

The psalmist, no doubt, looked far beyond His humble birth to His glorious reign: "Arise, O Lord, into thy rest; thou and the ark of thy strength. Let thy priests be clothed with righteousness; and let thy saints shout for joy" (verse 8, 9).

The answer to this prayer is found in God's response: "For the Lord hath chosen Zion; He hath desired it for His habitation. This is my rest forever: here will I dwell; . . . . I will also clothe her priests with salvation; and her saints will shout aloud for joy" (verses 13, 14, 16). "Behold, the tabernacle of God is with men, and He will dwell with them; (Revelation 21:3). "[He] hath made us kings and priests unto God and His Father; to Him be glory and dominion for ever and ever" (Revelation 1:6).

The basis of God's coming glorious kingdom, centered in the new Jerusalem but extending throughout the universe, is the coming of His Anointed into the world, to redeem and reclaim the world from the enemy. His "priests" can be "clothed with righteousness" (Revelation 19:8) because they have been first "clothed with salvation" (Isaiah 61:10). On the other hand, "His enemies will I clothe with shame" (verse 18).

He will surely "ordain a lamp for mine Anointed" (verse 17). "They need no candle, neither light of the sun." "The Lamb is the light thereof" (Revelation 22:5; 21:23).

This glorious future eternal kingdom can well occupy the thoughts and prayers of the people of God — all the more as they continue to grow in both physical and spiritual maturity. But this will not be because of selfish desires for peace and everlasting personal joys, but because we seek to desire that which God desires. And this, indeed, is why He created and redeemed His people, that He might have eternal fellowship with them in the New Jerusalem. "This is my rest for ever: here will I dwell; for I have desired it. I will abundantly bless her provision: I will satisfy her poor with bread" (verse 15).

Chapter 33

THE END OF THE JOURNEY
(Psalm 133)

In their long, upward trek to Jerusálem for the annual feasts, the pilgrims eagerly looked forward to the end of the journey. When they finally arrived, there would be great rejoicing and a wonderful spirit of unity with all the people of God who had converged on the city.

Just so will there be rejoicing and oneness when "we shall all be changed, In a moment, in the twinkling of an eye, at the last trump" (I Corinthians 15:52). Since we will be with the Lord Himself, we shall all become one in Him. "Till we all come in the unity of the faith, and of the knowledge of the Son of God, unto a perfect man, unto the measure of the stature of the fulness of Christ" (Ephesians 4:13).

Then will finally be fulfilled completely the prophecy of Psalm 133:1. "Behold, how good and how pleasant it is for brethren to dwell together in unity." In type it *should* be descriptive of each local congregation of believers, for they are "brethren," but in practice it is seldom found.

This beautiful unity is illustrated by a remarkable

simile, being compared to the fragrant anointing oil for the high priest, covering his head, his beard, and down over the skirts of his garments. Oil is well-known in Scripture as a symbol of God's Spirit, so in this case it speaks especially of unity produced by the Holy Spirit — "the unity of the Spirit in the bond of peace" (Ephesians 4:4). The only two occurrences of the word "unity" in the New Testament are these that have just been cited (Ephesians 4:4, 13), both fitting well the symbology of Psalm 133. There needs to be unity of both "the faith" and "the Spirit;" "speaking the truth in love" (Ephesians 4:15).

A like simile is used in the third verse. This pervasive unity is also compared to the dew on Mount Hermon and Mount Zion. As the anointing oil "descended on Aaron," from his head to his beard to his skirts, so the dew "descended" on Hermon and then "descended" on Zion. Thus, as the pilgrims had ascended to Jerusalem, so a spirit of unity had descended on them when they arrived. Just so, after we are "caught up together with them in the clouds, to meet the Lord in the air" (I Thessalonians 4:16), we shall soon see "that great city, the holy Jerusalem, descending out of heaven from God" (Revelation 21:10).

Mount Hermon is far in the north and is very lofty. Mount Zion is in the south and is much lower in elevation. Yet the same dew covered both, symbolizing the eventual unification of the northern and southern kingdoms and the pervasive presence of the Lord in all His people, no matter how exalted or how lowly.

The end of the journey for every believer is finally on Mount Zion. "But ye are come unto mount Sion, and unto the city of the living God, the heavenly Jerusalem" (Hebrews 12:22). There will then be no more divisions or dissensions. "For there the Lord commanded the blessing, even life for evermore" (verse 3).

Chapter 34

ETERNAL PRAISE AND BLESSING
(Psalm 134)

The last of the Songs of Degrees is also the shortest, but comprises in type the longest period of time, with its end in eternity. After the journey's end in glory, then must follow nothing but goodness forever — blessing from the Lord *to* His people and a blessing of the Lord in praise *by* His people.

These eternal praises were pictured in type by those in the temple who were responsible for its care and services during the night, indicating that God is particularly pleased with those whose hearts continue to praise Him even in the darkness. "It is a good thing to give thanks unto the Lord, and to sing praises unto thy name, O most High: To shew forth thy loving kindness in the morning, and thy faithfulness every night" (Psalm 92:1, 2). It was at midnight in a Philippian prison that "Paul and Silas prayed, and sang praises unto God" (Acts 16:25), an event which led to a miraculously-timed earthquake and the salvation of the keeper of the prison and his family.

In the New Jerusalem, of course, there will be "no

night there" (Revelation 22:5), as well as "no more death, neither sorrow, nor crying" (Revelation 21:4). Nevertheless, those who have learned to praise God even during times of sorrow and crying and death will be all the more able in eternity to "shew forth the praises of Him who hath called you out of darkness into His marvelous light" (I Peter 2:9). The possible implication of verse 2 is that it will be such as these who will be closest of all to the Lord's personal presence in eternity. "Lift up your hands *in the sanctuary,* and bless the Lord."

The final note of the Songs of Degrees is a beautiful invocation, looking back to the creation and forward to the consummation, recognizing God alone as the author of all blessing. He made all things in heaven and earth and finally will reconcile all things in heaven and earth (Colossians 1:20). With His throne in the New Zion (Revelation 22:1, 3), there shall be "no more curse" — only blessing forevermore! "The Lord that made heaven and earth bless thee out of Zion."

PART FIVE

THE PRAISE PSALMS
OF THE REDEEMED

Chapter 35

THE GREAT CONGREGATION

In Chapter I, the general structural organization of the book of Psalms was briefly examined, noting that it was composed of five "Books." The last five chapters, however, seem intended as an Epilogue to the entire book of Psalms. They form a fitting climax to this complete, wonderful "Book of Praises of Israel," as the book of Psalms has been known through the ages. We conclude our studies in the Psalms, therefore, with an exposition of these five remarkable psalms.

These chapters in the Epilogue might well be called the "Hallelujah Psalms." Each of them both begins and ends with this exhortation: "Praise ye the Lord." This command, however, is only one word in the Hebrew — "Hallelujah!"

The theme of praise for the Lord permeates the entire book of Psalms — as it should permeate the entire life of each man and woman — but it reaches its grand climax at the very end. These last five chapters describe nothing less than a great eternal fellowship of heavenly praise beginning at the end of this present age and continuing through the endless ages to come.

The words "praise," "praising," and similar forms occur more in the book of Psalms than in all other books of the Bible put together. But then, in Psalms 146-150 such words occur more than three times as often (44 times) as in any other five chapters, even in the book of Psalms (13 times in Psalms 115-119).

There are also a number of remarkable patterns associated with the concept of "praise" in the book of Psalms. The phrase "praise ye the Lord" (Hallelujah) occurs 22 times in the entire book (ten of them in these last five psalms), and this appropriately corresponds to the number of letters in the alphabet of the Hebrew language, the language in which God first revealed His Word to mankind (see also the discussion on this subject in the expositions of Psalm 22 and Psalm 119). The first occurrence is at the conclusion of the 104th Psalm, the greatest psalm on God's great works of creation and providence.

The key to the interpretation of these five psalms of praise, however, is found in Psalm 22:22, in which the first occurrence of *hallal* ("to praise") in the book of Psalms is found. There, at the very climax of His sufferings on the cross, these words are prophetically recorded as coming from the heart of Jesus Christ. "I will declare thy name unto my brethren: in the midst of the congregation will I praise thee."

That "congregation" was initially only the pitifully small band of believers grieving at the foot of the cross. This verse is quoted in Hebrews 2:12, however, and there the congregation is said to be the church. During his earthly ministry Jesus, likewise speaking of the church, had said: "For where two or three are gathered together in my name, there am I in the midst of them" (Matthew 18:17, 20). Each local assembly, where men are "gathered together" in His name, thus have His promise that He is "in the midst of the congregation," leading its praises before the Lord, as it were. All churches are represented by the seven churches of Revelation 2 and 3, symbolized by the seven golden candlesticks, and there John saw "in the midst of the seven golden candlesticks one like unto the Son of Man" (Revelation 1:13).

All of these local and temporal assemblies, however, are but types of the grand eternal assembly, when all those who have loved and served Christ through the ages will finally be gathered together before His throne. They all will unitedly praise the Lord forever. "But ye are come unto mount Sion, and unto the city of the living God, the heavenly Jerusalem, and to an innumerable company of angels, To the general assembly and church of the firstborn, which are written in heaven, and to God the judge of all, and to the spirits of just men made perfect, and to Jesus The mediator of the new covenant, and to the blood of sprinkling; that speaketh better things than that of Abel" (Hebrews 12:22-24).

The book of Revelation also speaks of either the same, or a similar, future assembly. "And I beheld, and I heard the voice of many angels round about the throne and the beasts and the elders: and the number of them was ten thousand times ten thousand, and thousands of thousands; Saying with a loud voice, Worthy is the Lamb that was slain to receive power, and riches, and wisdom, and strength, and honour, and glory, and blessing. And every creature which is in heaven, and on the earth, and under the earth, and such as are in the sea, and all that are in them, heard I saying, Blessing, and honour, and glory, and power, be unto Him that sitteth upon the throne, and unto the Lamb for ever and ever" (Revelation 5:11-13).

This heavenly assembly (or similar assemblies) is mentioned several times throughout the book of Revelation (7:9-12; 14:2-3; 15:2-4), and finally, at the climax of the judgment on the earth as Christ prepares to return in triumph, we hear a final heavenly exhortation to the assembled multitude to praise the Lord: "And after these things I heard a great voice of much people in heaven, saying, Alleluia; Salvation, and glory, and honour, and power, unto the Lord our God: For true and righteous are His judgments. . . . And a voice came out of the throne, saying, Praise our God, all ye his servants, and ye that fear Him, both small and great. And I heard as it were the voice of a great multitude, and as the voice of many waters, and as the voice of mighty thunderings, saying, *Alleluia*: for the Lord God omnipotent reigneth" (Revelation 19:1-6).

In this glorious passage which begins the 19th chapter of Revelation, the word *Alleluia* occurs four times (verses 1, 3, 4, 6), and these are the only times it occurs in the New Testament. It is the Hebrew *Hallelujah* ("praise ye the Lord") transliterated directly into the Greek New Testament. This fact confirms our inference that the great "Hallelujah Psalms" of the Epilogue to the book of Psalms should be understood primarily as a prophetic description of that coming day when all believers "shall be caught up together with them in the clouds, to meet the Lord in the air: and so shall we ever be with the Lord" (I Thessalonians 4:17). Then we shall not only be locally gathered together in His name in our respective churches, but will actually experience "the coming of our Lord Jesus Christ, and our gathering together unto Him" (II Thessalonians 2:1). As the divine judgments of the tribulation take place on earth, we shall be in His presence in the heavens above the earth, and the great events and testimonies described in Psalms 146-150 will begin to unfold.

Immediately after the mighty victory cry from the cross, where Christ had testified, "in the midst of the congregation will I praise thee," (Psalm 22:22), there is noted a change of person in the 22nd Psalm, from the first person to the second person. It is as though the Holy Spirit Himself interjects the exhortation: "Ye that fear the Lord, praise Him!" (verse 23).

To this exhortation, there is the thankful response in the last verses (25-31) of Psalm 22, again in the first person. It is no longer Christ speaking, however, but the believer, for whom He has just died on the cross. David, the author of the psalm, no doubt included himself, by faith, as such a believer. And note how his testimony begins: "My praise shall be of thee in the great congregation. I will pay my vows before them that fear Him. The meek shall eat and be satisfied; they shall praise the Lord that seek Him; your heart shall live for ever. All the ends of the world shall remember and turn unto the Lord; and all the kindreds of the nations shall worship before thee" (verses 25-27).

We, like David, can look forward to being gathered together in that great congregation, and we, like him, will have abundant opportunity there to express our praise and thanks to the Lord who saved us. We will join, first of all in a heavenly anthem, never sung before; "And they sung a new song, saying, thou art worthy to take the book, and to open the seals thereof: for thou wast slain, and hast redeemed us to God by thy blood out of every kindred, and tongue, and people, and nation; And hast made us unto our God kings and priests; and we shall reign on the earth" (Revelation 5:9, 10).

From this point on, it seems reasonable to infer that Psalms 146-150 supply a prophetic chronologic framework of the testimonies and events that will be taking place centered there in the heavenly assembly. The Lord Jesus Christ, the Lamb on the throne, will lead these testimonies of praise and will direct the great events both in heaven and on the earth below.

As we proceed to an examination of these remarkable psalms, we may note a tentative and partial outline of their essential respective themes, as follows:

Psalm 146:   Praises of Redeemed Individuals.
Psalm 147:   Praises of Redeemed Israel.
Psalm 148:   Praises of Redeemed Nature.
Psalm 149:   Praises for God's Righteous Judgments.
Psalm 150:   Praises Universal and Eternal.

Perhaps we may visualize the scene as a grand heavenly choir, with the Lord Jesus as leader. There is a section for the angels, one for the church, one for Israel, one for the animals, one for the inanimate creation. Every creature of God is there to join in the great fellowship of praise. As the great Director signals to one after the other, each responds in song and testimony.

Chapter 36

THE SONGS OF THE SAVED
(Psalm 146)

First of all, as the heavenly meeting of the great congregation gets under way, the baton points to the Church — that is, to the general assembly and church of the first-born, those individuals whose names are written in heaven and whose spirits have been perfected (Hebrews 12:23). "Praise *ye* the Lord" (Psalm 146:1).

And surely, each redeemed soul in that vast body of believers, no doubt numbering many "thousands of thousands," has much to praise Him for! Each will respond, perhaps first in unison and then, as opportunity affords in the ages to come: "Praise the Lord, O *my* soul!"

Such testimonies of praise from individuals redeemed by Christ's blood will continue for ever. "I will sing praises unto my God while I have any being." Perhaps each will give his individual testimony, recalling in retrospect his experiences on the earth. Though each person has had different experiences in detail, the same great themes will have underlain them all.

The great enemy of true salvation has always been

humanism, the belief that man can provide his own salvation. The futility of such a faith is clearly seen in the light of eternity. "Put not your trust in helpless man — even in great leaders and princes" (verse 3). Great philosophers have sought ways to comprehend and conquer the universe, but they soon die and their philosophies perish with them. With pitifully few exceptions, the thoughts of even great scientists and philosophers are forgotten soon after they die. How absurd then to study — especially to trust — these pitiful products of human wisdom, every one of which will eventually "come to nought" (I Corinthians 2:6).

In contrast, the redeemed soul has rejected all these human inventions and trusted the "God of Jacob," for *that* God is the only true God, the one "which made heaven, and earth, the sea, and all that therein is" (verse 6). He alone, the God of creation, knows and reveals the truth, and He "keepeth truth for ever." The word of God, which *is* truth, is "forever . . . settled in heaven" (Psalm 119:89), and does not perish like the philosophies of men.

Furthermore, He "executes judgment" (verse 7), and it is probably at this very gathering that "we must all appear before the judgment seat of Christ" (II Corinthians 5:10). Each redeemed soul will be able to testify how God has supplied every need, providing food and liberty, guidance and strength, loving those who are "righteous" in Him and who therefore "work righteousness" for Him.

There is still more for which these redeemed men and women can praise the Lord! Their old physical bodies will have been made new in the great resurrection. In the most literal sense, "the Lord openeth the eyes of the blind" and "raiseth them that are bowed down" (verse 8). "Behold I make all things new," says the Lord Jesus (Revelation 21:5), and the body of each redeemed individual "shall have put on immortality" (I Corinthians 15:54).

At the same time, "the way of the wicked He turneth

upside down" (verse 9), and those who have been redeemed can testify of this in a two-fold sense. They were once among the wicked themselves, but their lives have been transformed. Secondly, all opposition from the wicked has finally been swallowed up in victory, and "the Lord shall reign for ever" in the heavenly Zion. "Praise ye the Lord."

Chapter 37

THE REDEMPTION OF ISRAEL
(Psalm 147)

Many saved Jews will, of course, be among this redeemed multitude, as individual believers. But, in addition, God has promised that He will one day restore Israel and Jerusalem as His chosen nation on the earth itself.

The great accomplishment will probably be taking place on the earth as the assemblage at the throne observes it from the heavens. So the great congregation, especially the redeemed Israelites therein, are next called on to praise the Lord. For, they will sing, "The Lord doth build up Jerusalem; He gathereth together the outcasts of Israel. He healeth the broken in heart, and bindeth up their wounds . . . . Praise the Lord, O Jerusalem; praise thy God, O Zion. For He hath strengthened the bars of thy gates; He hath blessed thy children within thee. He maketh peace in thy borders, and filleth thee with the finest of the wheat . . . . He showeth His word unto Jacob, His statutes and His judgments unto Israel. He hath not dealt so with any nation; and as for His judgments, they have not known them. Praise ye the Lord" (verses 2-3; 12-14; 19-20).

When the promises were first made to Abraham, and then to Isaac and Jacob, they must have seemed impossible to fulfill. God had compared their progeny to the grains of sand and the stars of heaven (Genesis 22:17). Such a comparison must have seemed singularly inappropriate and inaccurate, since the number of sand grains was obviously infinitely greater than the 4,000 or so stars that could be seen in the heavens. Now, however, astronomers have calculated that the number of stars in the universe is indeed of the very order of magnitude (roughly 10^{25} in each case) as the number of grains of sand in the world. These cannot actually be counted, of course, but only sampled and estimated. God, however, created the stars, so "He telleth the number of the stars; He calleth them all by their names" (verse 4).

Adam was able to name the animals in part of a day, but how long would it take to name all the stars? If there are 10^{25} stars, and if one could name them at the rate of 3 per second, then it would take ten billion billion years (10^{19}) to "call them all by their names!"

It is obvious, therefore, that God named them all at once and therefore, He must be *omnipresent*. The next testimony (verse 5) recognizes that He is "of great power" — therefore, *omnipotent* and that "His understanding is infinite" — therefore, *omniscient*. Small wonder, therefore, that He is able both to prophesy and to accomplish the restoration of Israel and the complete fulfillment of His promises to His earthly people.

There is also another testimony in this psalm, affirming His control not only of the physical creation but also of the biological creation. There had already been one great physical judgment of the earth and its inhabitants, at the time of the great Flood, when the Lord had "cast the wicked down to the ground" (verse 6). But then, for that devastated world (in which, according to Genesis 2:5, there had never been any rain until the Flood came),

He had "covered the heaven with clouds, prepared rain
for the earth, made grass to grow on the newly-uplifted
mountains, and given food to the beasts and birds"
(verses 7-9). After that, following the Flood, there had
also come a great Ice Age in the northern latitudes. "He
giveth snow like wool: He scattereth the hoarfrost like
ashes. He casteth forth His ice like morsels: who can
stand before His cold" (verses 15-17).

But the great glaciers, like the waters of the Flood,
were also under His control. Soon tremendous peri-
glacial winds developed and the increasing plant life in
the lower latitudes sent their air-warming gases
(especially carbon dioxide) into the sky to be translated
aloft by the winds and to gradually restore a partial
greenhouse effect to the atmosphere, similar in kind
(but much less efficient) to that which had maintained
the warm, calm beautiful pre-Flood world. "He sendeth
out His word and melteth them; He causeth His winds
to blow, and the waters flow" (verse 18).

These testimonies of His control over the physical
world are woven in and out among the testimonies of His
power to fulfill His promises to Israel. The same Word
which could name the stars and command the elements
could surely accomplish the redemption of His people.
"He sendeth forth His commandment [the same word,
actually, as 'word' in verse 18] upon earth; His word runneth very swiftly" (verse 15).

And in the heart of this great testimony of God's
power both in creation and among the nations is the
assurance that His greatest joy is not in either one, "The
Lord taketh pleasure in them that fear Him, in those
that hope in His mercy" (verse 11).

Chapter 38
CREATION DELIVERED
(Psalm 148)

Having heard from redeemed mankind, both individually and nationally, the great praise Leader, turns
to His heavenly host: "Praise ye the Lord . . . . from the
heavens . . . in the heights. Praise ye Him, all His
angels: praise ye Him, all His hosts" (verses 1-2).

Angels are created beings, probably created on the
first of the six days of creation (see exposition of Psalm
104), and they "excel in strength" (Psalm 103:20). They
are "ministering spirits" for the "heirs of salvation"
(Hebrews 1:14) and so are interested in the progress of
God's plan of salvation, "which things the angels desire
to look into" (I Peter 1:12). It is highly fitting, therefore,
that this "innumerable company of angels" in the
heavenly assembly (Hebrews 12:22; Revelation 5:11)
should desire likewise to give their praises to the Lord.

But then, the exhortation is given even to the inanimate creation and to the animals also to praise the Lord.
Exactly how this can be done we do not yet understand,
but the same God who made them is the one who gives
the commandment, so He will enable them somehow to

do so. Certainly in their beauty and order and in the accomplishment of their respective purposes, they speak eloquently even now of God's power and wisdom. "The heavens declare the glory of God" (Psalm 19:1); "the stones immediately cry out" (Luke 19:40); "the lightnings go and say unto thee, Here we are" (Job 38:35); "the seven thunders uttered their voices" (Revelation 10:3).

However, in the present order of things, "the whole creation groaneth and travaileth in pain together until now" (Romans 8:21), and its deliverance from this bondage of corruption is likewise awaiting Christ's work of redemption and His victory over sin and death. It was created "very good" (Genesis 1:31), and the fulfillment of God's purpose in creation requires that it be restored to this original condition. Someday there will be "no more curse" (Revelation 22:3) on the ground, and He will "make all things new" (Revelation 21:5).

When the assembly is gathered in heaven, changes will begin to take place on the earth and in the heavens which will culminate in complete restoration of all to their primeval perfection, which will then last forever. Accordingly, the various stars and all other created things can also join in praise to the Lord, both in retrospect and prospect, looking back to the primeval creation and forward to the restored and eternal creation.

First, the sun and moon and stars praise the Lord, with the heavens (atmospheric, stellar, and angelic) in which they function. Also the "waters above the heavens" have evidently been raised from the earth up into the skies, restoring the ancient "waters above the firmament" (Genesis 1:7) which had maintained the ideal environment in the original world. This will probably be accomplished, at least in part, by the great physical upheavals that will have taken place during the Great Tribulation period on earth when there will be neither rains nor winds (Revelation 11:6; 7:1), but great solar heat (Revelation 16:8) and consequent vaporizing of the lakes and oceans.

Note also the testimony of fiat creation in verse 5. "He commanded, and they were created." True creation is instantaneous. "He spake, and it was done" (Psalm 33:9). Likewise, note the assertion that they would last forever. "He hath also stablished them for ever and ever: He hath made a decree which shall not pass." The idea that this present universe will cease to exist at the judgment day is not the teaching of Scripture. God had a purpose in creating every star, and that purpose would hardly be served by annihilating them. "I know that, whatsoever God doeth, it shall be for ever: nothing can be put to it, nor anything taken from it: and God doeth it, that men should fear before Him" (Ecclesiastes 3:14). See also Psalms 78:69; 104:5; Ecclesiastes 1:4; Daniel 12:3; etc.

Then the earth also is exhorted to praise the Lord, with all its systems and processes — deeps and mountains and hills, fire and hail, snow and evaporation, as well as the great winds. Most of these systems were not operative in the primeval world, becoming active as agents of judgment when sin came in, and especially during and after the Flood. They would still be utilized during the period of great tribulation, taking place on earth while the great assembly was convening in heaven, even though ultimately, in the new earth, there would be no further need for them. Nevertheless, in their immediate function as manifestations and implementations of God's judgment, they were, indeed, praising the Lord. Then attention turns to the plants and animals. The fruit trees and timber trees were to praise the Lord. So were the beasts and cattle, creeping things and birds, even the "dragons" (verse 7). This looks back in retrospect to the original creation of the animals on the fifth and sixth days of creation. The dragons (Hebrew *tannin*) were the same as the "sea monsters" or "great whales" of Genesis 1:21; in all probability, such monsters of the deep still live in modern oceans and deep inland lakes. They will evidently still be living on the earth at the time when the great congregation is gathered in heaven, and so will also be able to add their testimony to God's praise.

The animal kingdom will continue to exist during the earth's great millennial period, but all enmity between man and the animals will have been removed, with harmony prevailing as in the original creation (Isaiah 11:6-9; 65:24, 25). In the new earth, however, there will be "no more sea" (Revelation 21:1), so that at least sea animals will evidently cease to exist as well, their purpose having been completed. Whether or not there will be terrestrial animals on the new earth, the Scriptures do not say specifically, but such references as this one, in addition to Isaiah 65:24, 25, as well as the general concept of the originally-created fellowship between Adam and the animals he named, make such a thing appear at least possible. If so, of course, they would have to be newly-created, not the products of resurrection or reproduction of animals in a previous age.

And finally there is a call to all those people yet on the earth — kings of the earth, judges of the earth (note Psalm 2:10), young men and young women, old men and children. "Let *them* praise the name of the Lord." There is still time and room, even for these. Both during the tribulation period and the millennium, there will be people on the earth, in the flesh, needing salvation. The redeemed and resurrected saints in the heavenlies will eagerly hope that those below will respond to the call of the Spirit to come to Christ, whose "name alone is excellent" and whose "glory is above the earth and heaven." Of all those yet on the earth, the people of reviving Israel are His greatest concern, and the psalm concludes with another special testimony of and to them. "He also exalteth the horn of his people . . . the children of Israel, a people near unto Him. Praise ye the Lord."

Chapter 39

PRAISE THROUGH GOD'S JUDGMENTS
(Psalm 149)

Neither God nor His people find any pleasure in the death of the wicked (Ezekiel 33:11), and God is long-suffering, not willing that any should perish (II Peter 3:9). Nevertheless, He is also a just God and sin, when it is finished, must bring forth death (James 1:15). God's judgments, as well as His mercy, bring glory to His name: "Fear God, and give glory to Him; for the hour of His judgment is come" (Revelation 14:7). After the praises from redeemed believers, redeemed Israel, and nature in the first three of the Hallelujah Psalms, the emphasis in this psalm is on praising God for His righteous judgments on the earth. In God's omnipotence, He is able even to make man's rebellious wickedness an occasion for good. "Surely the wrath of man shall praise thee: the remainder of wrath shall thou restrain" (Psalm 76:10).

After the initial "Hallelujah," the first exhortation is to "sing a new song." The word "song" occurs more in the book of Psalms than in all the rest of the Bible put together. Similarly there are six "new songs" in Psalms

(33:3; 40:3; 96:1; 98:1; 144:9; 149:1), and only three in the rest of the Bible (Isaiah 42:10, Revelation 5:9; 14:3). Evidently, all believers in heaven sing this new song; but there is a special exhortation to the children of Israel to rejoice in their great King, Messiah.

The great joy is apparently because of the imminent return of Christ to the earth, when the "children of Zion" shall finally receive the promise of the Messianic kingdom. The saints are joyful in the glory in contemplation of His promise that "the meek shall inherit the earth" (Matthew 5:5). "For the Lord taketh pleasure in His people; He will beautify the meek with salvation" (verse 4).

The day is near, when heaven will be opened and the armies in heaven will follow Christ to make war against the armies of the kings of the earth (Revelation 19:11-19). This is evidently the meaning of the next verses: "Let the high praises of God be in their mouth, and a two-edged sword in their hands: To execute vengeance upon the heathen, and punishments upon the people; To bind their kings with chains, and their nobles with fetters of iron, To execute upon them the judgment written" (verses 6-9).

It is important always to interpret Scripture in proper context. Unfortunately, the above verses have been badly misused, especially during the wars of the Reformation, with both Protestants and Catholics using them to justify warfare and persecution in the name of Christ. As we have seen, however, the context is really prophetic, looking forward to the great war of Armageddon and the judgment of the nations.

It is indeed true, however, that the redeemed will take part in God's final judgment on the wicked. "Do you not know that the saints will judge the world? . . . . know ye not that we shall judge angels?" (I Corinthians 6:2, 3). "And he that overcometh, and keepeth my works unto the end, to him will I give power over the nations; And he shall rule them with a rod of iron; as the vessels of a potter shall they be broken to shivers; even as I received of

my Father" (Revelation 2:26, 27). "And the kingdom
and dominion, and the greatness of the kingdom under
the whole heaven shall be given to the people of the
saints of the most High" (Daniel 7:27). "And I saw
thrones, and they sat upon them, and judgment was
given unto them: . . . and they lived and reigned with
Christ a thousand years" (Revelation 20:4).

Whether we understand or not and whether we agree
or not, the fact remains that we are now being prepared
for just such a ministry in the age to come. The resurrected believer will in that day have been made like
Christ (I John 3:2; Romans 8:29), in hatred of sin as well
as love of righteousness, and thus will be fully capable of
participating with Him in judgment.

Chapter 40

UNIVERSAL PRAISE

(Psalm 150)

This final psalm looks far ahead to the grand consummation, after all rebellion and wickedness have been purged from God's creation, the curse has been removed from the earth, and Satan cast forever into the lake of fire. The heavenly Jerusalem and its inhabitants have already enjoyed the presence of the Lord throughout the seven years of great tribulation on earth, the thousand years of peace while Satan was confined in the abyss, the final rebellion of Gog and Magog and the judgment of the great white throne. Then the holy city had come down out of heaven to the renewed earth, all things in heaven and earth had finally been gathered together as one in Christ and the dispensation of the fulness of times (Ephesians 1:10) had begun. These great events are described in Revelation 19-20.

The time will then finally have arrived for the grandest doxology of all. God's plan of salvation has been completely accomplished and the whole creation is "very good" again and forever.

"Praise ye the Lord." The cry goes forth from the great

Leader of all praises, the Lord Jesus, and the universe begins to echo His praise. It begins in its center, in the very throne in the New Jerusalem. "Praise God in His sanctuary."

From there it surges forth in all directions. "Praise Him in the firmament of His power." The "firmament" (Hebrew *raqia*) means, literally, "stretching out," so that the command is actually to praise the Lord in the stretching-out of His power. His power, of course, stretches out infinitely through all space, so the angelic songs of praise likewise stretch out to the infinite recesses of God's creation.

Verse 1 has outlined the extent of the praises; verse 2 outlines their themes. God is to be praised both for His mighty acts and for His excellent greatness — what He does and what He is. His great work of creation had already been praised by the assembly in Revelation 4:11 and His greater work of redemption in Revelation 5:9. The "abundance of His greatness" must be nothing less than the glory which the Lord had longed for His disciples to see when He spoke to His Father in the upper room (John 17:24). Finally they have all "seen Him as He is" (I John 3:2, 3), and joyous songs of praise sound forth from all the redeemed and purified.

Verses 3, 4, and 5 describe *how* to praise the Lord, as verse 1 tells *where* and verse 2 says *why*. There will evidently be an abundance of musical instruments in the new Jerusalem. The heavenly assembly was already experienced in the playing of harps (Revelation 5:8; 14:2; 15:2), and these will be joined by many others. Wind instruments (trumpets, organs), stringed instruments (psaltery, harp, and others), and percussion instruments (timbrel, loud cymbals, high-sounding cymbals) will all provide a glorious musical background for the universal songs of praise. The music will also serve as accompaniment for joyful and expressive dancing (verse 4). This will not be sensuous dancing, of course, but dancing which is appropriate as a testimony to the glory and grace of God. "Thou hast turned for me my mourning into dancing: thou hast put off my sack-cloth, and girded me with gladness; To the end that my glory may sing praise to thee, and not be silent. O Lord my God, I will give thanks unto thee for ever" (Psalm 30:11, 12). "Let them praise His name in the dance: let them sing praises unto Him with the timbrel and harp" (Psalm 147:3).

And finally, as the music and singing and dancing resound in ever-expanding waves of joy from the sanctuary and throughout the universe, the climactic exhortation peals forth: "Let everything that hath breath praise the Lord!" The word "breath" (Hebrew *ruach*) is actually the same word as "Spirit," so this command may well be a reference to the universal presence of God's Holy Spirit in all His Creation.

Then the book of Psalms ends where eternity begins, with the universal shout: "Hallelujah!"

Other Books By Henry M. Morris

Available from Creation-Life Publishers
P.O. Box 15666
San Diego, California 92115

Scientific Creationism

The most comprehensive, documented exposition of all the scientific evidences dealing with origins, showing clearly the superiority of the creation model over the evolution model. Public school edition contains no Biblical or religious material; intended especially as a reference handbook for teachers.

General Edition (includes Biblical documentation)

No. 140, Kivar $4.95

Public School Edition (non-religious text)

No. 141, Kivar $5.95; No. 357, Cloth $7.95

The Genesis Record
A Scientific and Devotional Commentary on the Book of Beginnings

Written as a narrative exposition, this complete commentary on the book of Genesis stresses both the scientific integrity and historical accuracy of every chapter. The author is both a scientist and Bible teacher of long experience, providing unusual insights and character studies not available in other commentaries, along with thorough treatment of all problem passages. Contains complete indexes and several helpful appendixes and maps. 708 pages. No. 070, Cloth $12.95

Many Infallible Proofs

Published in 1975, this valuable book has already demonstrated its effectiveness in strengthening the faith of new Christians and convincing the serious non-Christian, in church and home study classes in defense of the faith and effective witnessing, and as a complete textbook for college courses in Apologetics or Christian Evidences. Contains factual evidences and sound reasoning supporting the foundational truths of God's Word.

No. 102, Kivar $4.95; No. 103, Cloth $6.95

The Bible Has The Answer
Co-authored with Martin E. Clark, Ed.D.

This enlarged edition of the popular classic by Dr. Morris provides logical Bible-based answers to 150 questions dealing with the most common and vexing problems of the Bible and the Christian life. On those few questions dealing with doctrinal issues, orientation is pre-millennial and Baptistic; on all others it is non-denominational.

No. 023, Paper $4.95

The Troubled Waters of Evolution

The most complete account, from a Biblical and creationist point of view, of the long history of evolutionary thought, with a non-technical study of the evidence for creation, especially the second law of thermodynamics.

No. 170, Paper $2.95

The Remarkable Birth of Planet Earth

An introductory study of the biblical and scientific evidence for the special creation of the world and of God's continuing control and concern. Covers the amazing order of the universe, early history of all mankind, delusion of evolution, the worldwide flood, and many other historical and prophetic confirmations of God's handiwork.

No. 131, Paper $1.50

Education For The REAL World

Stresses the necessity for a *biblically-based* education in every area of study, rather than a secular education in a Christian surrounding. A book every parent, pastor, teacher, and school administrator should read.

No. 053, Paper $3.95

The Scientific Case for Creation

This book focuses its attention on the scientific evidence *for* creation. The average reader can comprehend the concepts, and the mathematical substantiation is furnished for the person who wishes to verify them for himself. Concentrates on the scientific, rather than the theological aspects of creation. Two-color throughout.

No. 139, Paper $1.95

The Genesis Flood

Co-authored with John C. Whitcomb, Th.D.

The most comprehensive scientific exposition of creation and the flood. Demonstrates the inadequacies of uniformitarianism and evolution and presents an abundance of pertinent scientific data supporting creationism and catastrophism. Thoroughly documented and indexed.

No. 069, Kivar $5.95

The Twilight of Evolution

A summary of the impact of evolution of modern life, as well as its ultimate end. Concise scientific documentation for special creation and the world-wide flood.

No. 172, Paper $1.95

That You Might Believe

A new edition of the first book ever written by Dr. Morris. This evangelistic presentation of Christian evidences has been used to win many people to Christ. This updated edition should prove even more effective in today's world.

No. 168, Paper $4.50

Other Books of Interest

Available from Creation-Life Publishers
P.O. Box 15666
San Diego, California 92115

EVOLUTION? The Fossils Say NO!

Duane T. Gish, Ph.D.

The fossil record proves there has been no evolution in the past and none in the present, conclusively documented in this critique. Many photos. With over 100,000 in print in this version, this book is now also available in a Public School Edition with a non-religious text.

No. 054, Paper $1.95

Public School Edition　　　No. 055, Paper $2.95

DINOSAURS, Those Terrible Lizards

Duane T. Gish, Ph.D.

Illustrated by Marvin Ross

At last! A book for young people, from a creationist perspective, on those intriguing dinosaurs. No one living in the world today has ever seen a real live dinosaur—but did people in earlier times live with dinosaurs? Were dragons of ancient legends really dinosaurs? Does the Bible speak about dinosaurs? The answers are in this book! Written by Dr. Gish, noted scientist who is author of the best seller *EVOLUTION? The Fossils Say NO!,* this book is profusely illustrated in color on beautiful 9" x 11" pages.　　　　　　　　　　　　　　No. 046, Cloth $5.95

Explore The Word!

Henry M. Morris, III, D. Min.

A new approach to Bible study. This book will prove a most beneficial aid to all who are sincerely interested in studying to show themselves approved in the knowledge and use of God's Word. *Explore the Word!* is a unique book designed to fill the gap between the many layman's study helps and the complex theoretical hermeneutic books. It is directed to the inquisitive Christian who wants to research God's truths without complete dependence upon the teachings of others. Makes possible an independence for personal study seldom experienced by the Christian. No. 056, Paper $5.95

The Moon: Its Creation, Form, and Significance

John C. Whitcomb, Th.D.

Authoritative information on earth's closest space neighbor. "This book presents the best comparison of the various moon origin theories I have ever seen."—Jim Irwin, Apollo 15 Astronaut. 16 pages of color photos.

No. 105, Cloth $7.95

Creation: Acts/Facts/Impacts

Ed. by Henry M. Morris, Duane T. Gish, George M. Hillestad

This book is a compilation of the important articles and reports on debates that appeared in ICR's ACTS & FACTS for 1972 and 1973, including the Impact Series No. 1-9. Contains helpful information not available from any other source. No. 037, Paper $2.95

The Battle for Creation

Ed. by Henry M. Morris, Ph.D. and Duane T. Gish, Ph.D.

More fascinating articles from ICR's ACTS & FACTS from 1974 and 1975, including complete Impact Series for that period. Subjects include "The Great Debate," "Creation Goes to College," "Creation and the Public Schools," and many others. No. 013, Paper $3.95

Up With Creation!

Ed. by Donald Rohrer and Duane T. Gish, Ph.D.

Third in the popular series chronicling the ongoing creation/evolution controversy. Includes Impact Series from ICR's ACTS & FACTS 1976 and 1977.

No. 179, Paper $3.95

ORIGINS: Two Models

Richard Bliss, M.S., Ed.D.

A module for use in Jr. and Sr. High Schools, examining

origins. Planned for 3 weeks of study, the scientific models for both creation and evolution are presented. Working questions and many illustrations help explain the subject matter. A glossary of definitions runs throughout the book, which also includes an extensive bibliography. 8½" x 11".

ORIGINS: Two Models, No. 114, Paper $3.95
Christian Teacher's Guide, No. 115, Paper $1.50
Public School Teacher's Guide, No. 116, Paper $1.50
Christian Overhead Transparencies, No. 117, $17.00
Public School Overhead Transparencies, No. 118, $17.00
Christian Set, No. 119, $20.00 (1 book, T. guide, transparencies)
Public School Set, No. 120, $20.00 (1 book, T. guide, transparencies)

Origin of Life

R. Bliss, M.S., Ed.D. Gary E. Parker, M.S., Ed.D.

An open and objective approach to the origin of living things. Deals with experiments and criticisms of significant efforts by scientists working in this field.

No. 121, Paper $3.95

Streams of Civilization

Albert Hyma, Ph.D. and Mary Stanton, Ed.D.

Ancient History to 1572 A.D. A world history text for junior and senior high schools. An all-inclusive, value-oriented presentation, blending archaeology, biology, philosophy, science, and the fine arts to clarify history. Creation and evolution are investigated as unbiased, scientific approaches to the origin of man and his universe. Over 350 illustrations, maps, and photographs, with a quick reference comprehensive index. 8½" x 11", 411 pages.

Textbook, No. 145, Cloth $12.95; Teacher's Guide, No. 146, Paper $2.50; Christian Supplement & Home Study Guide, No. 147, Paper $1.50